The Thompson Family: Untold Stories from the Past (1830-1960)

Dr. Walter B. Curry, Jr.

The Thompson Family:
Untold Stories from the Past (1830-1960)

Dr. Walter B. Curry, Jr.

Library of Congress Cataloging-in-Publication Data
Curry, Walter B., 1980-

ISBN: 9798709838970

For information on this publication, contact the author:
renaissancepublicationsllc@gmail.com or (803) 404-2117.

Printed in the United States of America

"Those who have no record of their forebears lose the inspiration which comes from the teaching of biography and history"- Carter G. Woodson

DEDICATION

This book is dedicated to the following individuals of the Thompson Family who are deceased, while living provided me vast, insightful information that contributed to the contents of this book.

Viola "Babe" Williams Thompson
Lumanda Thompson Williams
Levi Quattlebaum
Otis Corbitt
Wallace Seawright, Jr.
Artee Quattlebaum Brown
Calvin Thompson
R.D. Thompson
Catherine Seawright McCollough
Floster T. Ellison, Jr.

Table of Contents

INTRODUCTION

During the early years of my childhood, my mother, Cheryl Seawright Curry, always spoke about her relatives. She shared many stories about her experiences with her parents, grandparents, aunts, uncles, cousins, who were vividly anecdotal. She showed me places where many of her relatives lived including her birthplace and immediate family; furthermore, she expressed that many of her siblings including herself, were named after several direct ancestors and other relatives.

One day I spent a weekend with my uncle, the late Wallace Seawright, Jr. who lived in Salley, South Carolina. As the oldest of my mother's siblings, he had wealth of information about my great-grandparents, the late Robert Lee and Alice Thompson Seawright. He instructed me to visit my grandfather's aunt, Viola "Babe" Thompson for more information. While shelling peas with Aunt Babe, she stated that my great-grandmother mother, Francis Coats Thompson, who she vividly described as a fast talking, stout woman. In addition, she stated that Purvis Thompson, Sr., who married Grandma Francis and was a first cousin to my great-great-grandfather Oscar J. Thompson, Sr., helped raised my great-grandmother. The highlight of the visit was Aunt Babe showing me their pictures.

I followed up my inquiry when I was a congressional intern in Washington, DC during the summer of 2001. At that time, my great-grandmother sister, Lumanda Thompson Williams was living in New York. New York was only 4 hours away from DC, so I decided to take a bus trip there to spend a weekend with her. One of her daughters showed me a book, the old Thompson Family History book, a souvenir of the 1987 Thompson Family Reunion that took place in Washington, DC. The book is very diverse with pictures, a few narratives, and a family tree. From that moment, my interest in learning more about the family piqued.

A few years later, I visited my senior cousin, Artee Quattlebaum Brown. Affectionately known as "Cousin Art", I did not know how we were kin until she revealed that her grandmother, Charlotte Quattlebaum, maiden name was "Thompson". Then she revealed that her grandmother and my adopted great-great-grandfather, Purvis Thompson, Sr. were siblings. She remembered as a young girl, her grandmother always visited Purvis and his family. Hungry for more knowledge, I reached out to my cousin, Wayne Quattlebaum, the great-grandson of Charlotte Quatttlebaum, who suggested that I attend the Quattlebaum Family Reunion to learn more about the family. I along with my uncle, Ronnie Seawright, attended the event in Durham, North Carolina. There I met two senior cousins and Charlotte's granddaughters, Christine Quattlebaum Morgan and Annie Laurel Quattlebaum Jackson, both sisters, who told the story about how their grandmother father, Milledge Thompson, born into slavery purchased his freedom. Later, he secured the freedom of their grandmother and her sister. While I have read stories about slaves acquiring their freedom through various means but being related to someone who did it, is more meaningful.

Another epiphany for me occurred when I spoke to my grandfather's first cousin, Calvin Thompson, who lived in Capitol Heights, Maryland. He stated that our direct ancestor, Lavinia Corley Thompson, served as cook in the Confederate Army. Not only she served but applied for a state pension for her service and was approved. At the time, I did not believe any African American served in the Confederacy. He sent me the documentation of her service. As I read it, I concurred that her service was indeed historic and should be honored.

The accounts along with other accounts were the impetus for me to chronicle the diverse narratives that reflect the experiences of my ancestors and their relatives. The zeal was further heightened when my cousin, Toretha Corley Wright, the granddaughter of Joshua and Queen Thompson Corley, birthed the idea of a family history book. After careful thought, prayer, and encouragement from family and friends, I decided it was time to move forward. Acknowledging the significance of genealogical history relative of my African ancestry in

2

traditional meanings, I know that the key to understanding the great mystery of self is to know who you are genealogically. My African ancestry informs that genealogy is critical in understanding the nature of a collective group of people of direct kinships known as "family".

The genealogical accounts have culminated into a treatise that chronicles the reflections and experiences of my ancestors and relatives. This book *The Thompson Family: Untold Stories of the Past (1830-1960)* is the first of several volumes that chronicles the genealogical epoch of the Thompson Family.

Research Methods

The objective in gathering information was to document the narratives through written historical data, personal experiences, and interviews-oral and written-with those who were familiar with the individuals in this book. The contents of this book are aligned with the *Genealogical Proof Standard* (GPS) ascribed by the Board for Certification of Genealogists.[1] [2] The constituents of the standard ensure that family histories are accurate and reflect historical reality as closely as possible. Secondary sources were consulted as well.

Genealogical Epoch Theoretical Framework

While there is no mainstream standardized theoretical framework to informed genealogical research, I contemplated the imperativeness of a theoretical framework for the necessity of bringing out the "liveliness" of the individuals portrayed in the narratives by centering on the meaning of epoch. The word "epoch" means a period in a person's life defined by notable events or particularly characteristics that define a person's life. Milestones, virtues, transgressions, shortcomings, in addition to eventful historical and cultural contexts ascribes a person's epoch.

---

[1] The Board of Certification of Genealogists is a body of genealogists that promote the highest standards of competence and ethics among genealogists and thereby foster public confidence in genealogy as a respectable and respected research discipline and field of study.

[2] See *Genealogical Standards* by the Board of Certification of Genealogists.

The exposition resulted in the coining of the genealogical epoch theoretical framework. This framework posits that ancestors and relatives are not nominally restricted by name but are "epoch beings" expressing their behavior and thinking. In other words, ancestors and relatives are namely identified denoted by their character and life experiences.

Organization of the Book

The body of the book is organized into three chapters. The Genesis, Narrative Essays, and Narrative Analyses.

The "Genesis" briefly explains the progenitor origin of the Thompson Family, their lineage of leadership at Smyrna Missionary Baptist Church, and the dissemination of relatives. The Narrative Essays are detailed accounts of unique individuals of the Thompson Family. These individuals were chosen based on litany of archived information. The Narrative Analyses are detailed summaries that goes beyond the factual representation of genealogical narratives.

The Appendixes consist of documentation (i.e., pictures, primary sources).

THE GENESIS

According to the 1987 Thompson Family Reunion book, Samuel and Phyliss Thompson had seven male children: Milledge Thompson (the oldest), Pharaoh Thompson, Evan Thompson, Daniel Thompson, Anderson Thompson, Louis Thompson, and Logan Thompson. The place of origin from whence they came is unknown, but only Milledge, Louis, Logan, and Anderson settled in the area known as the "Skillet" community, located outside of Salley, South Carolina.[3]

Many relatives of the Thompson Family were members of Smyrna Missionary Baptist Church located near Springfield, South Carolina. Milledge, his son Otis Thompson, Sr., and sons-in-law, Isaac Quattlebaum, Lewis Miles, and Cain R. Scott, and James B. Livingston were the early deacons of the church.[4] [5] [6] Another son-in-law, James W. Kitchings, a graduate of Tuskegee University, was elected general manager to construct a new building for the church.[7] [8] [9] Logan was an ordained minister and both of his sons, Oscar J. Thompson, Sr. and Robert "Free" Thompson, and son-in-law, Jacob Rice were early deacons of the church.

From the early 1900's, many Thompson family relatives relocated for better employment and living opportunities. Some

---

[3]A philanthropist named Della Kitchings owned over 500 acres of wooded land. She told African Americans if they cleaned up the land during the first year, she would give them half of what they make. Some balked at the proposition because it was counterintuitive. They warned if African Americans acquiescence Della's proposition, they would be so hungry to a point of "licking a biscuit from a skillet".

[4] Isaac Quattlebaum married Milledge Thompson daughter, Charlotte Quattlebaum.

[5] Pollie Thompson Scott Miles, Milledge Thompson daughter, was married twice. Her first husband named Cain Scott and her second husband named Lewis Miles.

[6] James B. Livingston married Milledge Thompson daughter, Clara Livingston.

[7] James W. Kitchings married Milledge Thompson daughter, Louise Kitchings.

[8] Levi Quattlebaum, grandson of Isaac and Charlotte Thompson-Quattlebaum. Oral Interview, 2003, by Walter B. Curry, Jr. at Levi home in Williston, South Carolina.

[9] History of Smyrna Baptist Church (1873-1978).

moved northward mainly around the Washington, DC and New York City regions, some migrated to cities and rural areas across the South including South Carolina, and some moved westward. The current remnant of the Thompson family who lives in the Salley area the descendants of Milledge, Logan, and Anderson.

NARRATIVE ESSAYS

Milledge Thompson: A Freedman's Story

Milledge Thompson, the oldest of seven children, was born on October 5, 1830. His first wife, Laura Thompson, who was also a slave.[10] Out of their union, they had two daughters: Charlotte Thompson Quattlebaum and Clara Thompson-Livingston. Later in life, Laura was sold at a slave auction in Charleston, South Carolina to a slave owner around the Horry County area.[11][12] Remarkably, Milledge daughters were not sold. During his enslavement, Milledge was given the opportunity to earn wages to secure his freedom. With considerable help from local White residents, Milledge was able to purchase his own freedom, in addition to purchasing the freedom of his daughters, Charlotte and Clara.

Later in life, Milledge married his second wife, Amanda Friday. Out of their union, they had sixteen children: Sumpter Thompson, Aucklin Thompson-Hunt, Nancy Thompson-Johnson, Bessie Thompson-Stroman, Clara Thompson-Livingston, Louise Thompson-Kitchings, Mary Thompson, Purvis Thompson, Otis Thompson, Benjamin Thompson, Henry Thompson, Lewis Thompson, Obanion Thompson, Matthew Thompson, James Thompson, and Nathan Thompson. In addition, he had one stepson, Joseph Pitts Thompson, who was Amanda's son from a prior relationship, and another daughter, Polly Thompson-Scott-Miles, from a previous relationship. The family attended Smyrna Missionary Baptist Church where Milledge was ordained as a deacon. Later, Milledge purchased 100 acres

---

[10] Annie Laurel Quattlebaum-Jackson, granddaughter of Isaac and Charlotte Thompson-Quattlebaum. Oral Interview, 1 July 2016, by Walter B. Curry, Jr. at Annie's home in Washington, District of Columbia.

[11] Annie Laurel Quattlebaum-Jackson.

[12] Later in life, Milledge communicated with his wife Laura. She lived in Charleston, South Carolina.

of land for $2 per acre near Kitchings Mill area outside of Salley, South Carolina.[13] They settled and farmed for many years.

Milledge died on January 8, 1903, at the age of 73. Two years later, his wife Amanda died in 1905 at the age of 60. They are both buried at Smyrna Missionary Baptist Church.

---

[13] Telephone Conversation with Bernard Thompson, grandson of Sumpter and Fannie Stroman-Thompson, 11 November 2016, by Walter B. Curry, Jr.

Otis Thompson, Sr.: An Individual Who Had Many Vocations

Otis Thompson, Sr. was one of fifteen children born to Milledge and Amanda Friday-Thompson born in 1877 in Salley, South Carolina. At a young age, Otis joined Smyrna Missionary Baptist Church where he was ordained as a deacon. As a deacon, Otis was known for his gift of singing spirituals that he earned the nickname "Note".[14] During baptism processionals, Otis led worshippers to the pond near the church singing spirituals. Otis also participated in several church-sponsored civic activities that benefited the greater community.[15] On Sunday afternoon of May 12, 1935, Otis participated in an educational rally at Smyrna Missionary Baptist Church to raise money to rebuild Piney Grove School from the burning ashes, a school for African American children.[16][17]

When Otis was of age, he married Mary Ellen McKie, who was a Cherokee Indian.[18] Out of their union, twelve children were born: Dallas Thompson, Otis Thompson, Jr., Richard Thompson, Clyde Thompson, Blanton Thompson, Buice Thompson, F.M. Thompson, Ella Mae Thompson-Gantt, Blanche Thompson-Gantt-Carson, Mattie Thompson-Gantt, Betty Thompson-Simmons, and Maud Thompson-Brooks. The family purchased land in the Skillet community where they grew vegetables and raised livestock for many years.[19] They lived

---

[14] Telephone Conversation with Bernard Thompson, grandson of Sumpter and Fannie Stroman-Thompson, 11 November 2016, by Walter B. Curry, Jr.

[15] In-person conversation with Floster T. Ellison, Jr., grandson of Lewis Miles and step-grandson of Pollie Thompson-Miles, 15 January 2004, by Walter B. Curry, Jr. at Floster home in Columbia, South Carolina.

[16] Activities Among Colored Aikenites and Vicinity, Aiken, South Carolina, The Journal and Review, 15 May 1935, p.2, www.newspapers.com.

[17] Piney Grove Colored School was built in 1939 or 1940 in near the Kitchings Mill Community near what is now 506 Tabernacle Road. It was a two-room school for African-American students. It closed in 1954 when A.L Corbett High School opened for African-American students.

[18] Samuel Gantt and Jacqueline Carter, grandchildren of Otis and Mary E. Thompson. Oral Interview, 12 November 2017, by Walter B. Curry, Jr. at Samuel's home near Largo, Maryland.

[19] Samuel Gantt and Jacqueline Carter.

in a wooden house with holes in the ceiling. When it rained, they used pots and pans to catch the water.

Family life was very charismatic. Otis and Mary Ellen had very opposite personalities. Otis was a very humble and jovial. Bossy in nature, Mary Ellen ran the house. She was so bossy that sometimes Otis would tell her to "Shut your mouth, Mary Ellen". Nevertheless, Mary Ellen was not afraid of confrontation. An incident occurred one day when a white man approached her and said, "I want your children to work on my farm". Unapologetically, she replied, "These not your children, these my children".

Otis pursued entrepreneurial and employment opportunities to earn money to support his family. On September 29, 1941, he and his first cousin John Friday contracted with the Aiken Lumber Company to sell lumber on their property in the sum of $650.[20] During the summer months, Otis would leave home and work in Washington, DC.[21] He was employed at a local grocery warehouse delivering groceries to different places around the city.[22] Otis was also employed at Sanitary (now Safeway) in located in Southwest DC working at the loading docks.[23] Occasionally, Mary Ellen and the children stayed with him in DC. While there, Mary Ellen contracted gall stones and had them removed. A physician by the name of Dr. Nelson performed the surgery on her. Later, Mary Ellen died in 1938 at the age of 56.

After Mary Ellen death, Otis continued to farm while his grown children, some married with their own families, left Salley and moved to Washington, DC. Later, Otis got sick and moved there to stay with his daughter, Blanch and her family. Otis died in 1956. Otis and his wife are buried next to each other at Smyrna Missionary Baptist Church.

---

[20] Timber Title from John Friday and Otis Thompson to Aiken Lumber Company, 10 September 1940 (filed 29 September 1941), Aiken County, South Carolina, Title Book No.75, p.243, Clerk of Court for Aiken County.
[21] 1930; Census Place: Washington, District of Columbia; Page: 13B; Enumeration District: 0256; digital image, Ancestry.com, assessed June 10, 2018, www.ancestry.com.
[22] 1930; Census Place: Washington, District of Columbia.
[23] Ibid.

The Vigilante Exploits of Murry Quattlebaum

Murry Quattlebaum, the youngest out of thirteen children born to Isaac and Charlotte Thompson-Quattlebaum, was born on March 18, 1896, in Salley, South Carolina. At a young age, he joined Smyrna Baptist Church. He later married Georgie Quattlebaum. Out of their union, four children were born: Grace Quattlebaum-Williams, Albert Quattlebaum, Murline Quattlebaum-Friday, and Joe Louis Quattlebaum. When Murry brother Alex Quattlebaum and his wife Joyce Quattlebaum passed away in the late 1920's, Murry took his brothers' children and raised them.[24]

On Friday May 20, 1922, Murry's brother was wanted for mortgaging a cow that did not belong to him but another family member.[25] The bill was given to Hays & Shull of Wagener, South Carolina and the case was turn over to the Wagener Police.[26] The police chief, Luke Rodgers, accompanied by Constable Norris Johnson of Magistrate Garvin's Court, had a warrant to arrest Murry's brother. Murry who was suspicious of the matter, asked Constable Johnson to show the warrant. Not satisfied with the response, Murry raised his gun to his shoulder and fired directly at Chief Rodgers shooting him in the stomach, jumping behind a mule as he discharged the weapon. Several shots were fired by Constable Johnson, but Murry darted off through the woods. Chief Rodgers, mortally wounded, was taken to Columbia to Baptist Hospital on Friday evening with the hope of possibly saving his life by an operation, through Dr. Brodie of Wagener stated his recovery would be almost a miracle. Chief Rodgers miraculously survived and was granted permission to leave the hospital the next day

---

[24] In-person conversation with Artee Quattlebaum Brown, granddaughter of Isaac and Charlotte Thompson-Quattlebaum, 15 June 2008, by Walter B. Curry, Jr. at Artee's home in Salley, South Carolina.

[25] Negro Wounds Wagener Police, Aiken, South Carolina, Aiken Standard, 25 October 1922, p.3, www.newspapers.com.

[26] Ibid.

and return to his home.[27] Chief Rodgers was still in critical condition from the effects of his wound and was unable to perform his duties as guardian of the peace for some time to come.[28]

There was an organized manhunt which included local citizens accompanied with bloodhounds to capture Murry. Near midnight Friday evening, Murry surrendered with his two brothers to Mr. W.H. Brodie who turned him over to Sheriff Howard. Coroner Tarver was entrusted with supervising Murry who was kept in irons, and he was safely placed in the Aiken jail. Shortly after midnight, Sheriff Howard deemed it best to have him taken to Columbia and placed in the state penitentiary, which was done by Deputy Noikie Robinson and Chief of Police Seth Busbee; the trio arriving at the penitentiary about 3 o'clock Saturday morning. While Sheriff Howard knew about Murry's surrender, Mr. Brodie was kept in entire ignorance of his whereabouts or through the intention of officers to secure him by Murry's brothers. A few days later, Murry posted bail in the sum of $1,200 before Magistrate Garvin in the Aiken Courthouse. Mr. Hampton Brodie going on his bond.[29]

In explanation his act, Murry stated that he had his gun across his arm returning from a squirrel hunt and that the weapon pointed at Chief Rodgers, who when he saw it, began shooting at him who replied nervously before he realized the weight of his action. This tale was offset by several witnesses who heard the gun fire first before the revolver shots were heard.[30]

On Wednesday May 9, 1923, three convicts, Murry Quattlebaum, Press Pickney, and Herbert Lindsey escaped from the

---

[27] Luke Rodgers Recovering, Aiken, South Carolina, Aiken Standard, 15 November 1922, p.1, www.newspapers.com.

[28] Luke Rodgers Recovering, p.1.

[29] Local Brevites, Aiken, South Carolina, Aiken Standard, 29 November 1922, p.3, www.newspapers.com.

[30] Ibid.

Aiken County chain gang at Whitlaw's Crossing late Sunday night.[31][32] Rewards were offered for each one of them by county officials.[33] Mr. W.B. Brodie, foreman of the Grand Jury informed folks that Murry turned himself in at Bell's Camp at 3 o'clock on Tuesday morning, May 15, 1923.[34] Murry stated that the other two convicts induced him to escape and after it was over, he decided that the best thing for him to do was to go back. Murry stated that Press Pinckney went to his aunt's house in Kitchings Mill to obtain food, and that he was going from there to see his mother who lives on Mr. Brodie's place.

Later in life, Murry Quattlebaum moved to Jamaica, New York. He died on April 13, 1972, at the age of 76. Murry is buried at Smyrna Missionary Baptist Church.

---

[31] Three Convicts Escape, Aiken, South Carolina, The Journal and Review, 9 May 1923, p.1, www.newspapers.com.

[32] Whitlaw's Crossing was located near present-day North Augusta, South Carolina.

[33] Three Convicts Escape, p.1.

[34] Ibid.

Tragedy in the Skillet: The Murder of Young Governor "Mint" Thompson, Jr.

Governor Hayes Thompson, Sr. was one of five children born to Rev. Logan and Lavinia Corley-Thompson on October 11, 1884, in Salley, South Carolina. At a young age, Governor joined Smyrna Missionary Baptist Church. In 1906, Governor married Sustanchia Henderson. Out of their union, six children were born: Robert Byrice Thompson, Effie Thompson, Essie Thompson-Martin, Governor "Mint" Thompson, Jr., Dorothy Thompson, and Cleola C. Calder.

On midnight Sunday, March 13, 1921, an unusual incident occurred.[35] George Piper, member of an industrious and prominent African-American family, became wildly intoxicated from moonshine began shooting up the neighborhood around Chapman Baptist Church in the Skillet community.[36] [37] Piper went so far as to shoot in to his father's house in his drunkenness.[38] Governor, who was Piper friend, took him to task for his conduct and Piper turned on him to shoot him, but Governor shot first, the bullets hitting Piper in the mouth and breast. Because of the wounds, Piper died.[39]

On Monday March 14, 1921, Governor surrender to the Sheriff at the courthouse being taken there by Mr. John D. Brodie. He was charged with murder and appeared before the court the following Tuesday.[40] Solicitor Gunter and William M. Smoak aided in the prosecution of the case and Messrs, Salley, and Gyles were Governor's

---

[35] Governor Thompson Shoots George Piper to Death Near Kitchings Mill, Aiken, South Carolina, The Journal and Review, 16 March 1921, p.1, www.newspapers.com.

[36] Governor Thompson Shoots George Piper to Death Near Kitchings Mill, p.1.

[37] Chapman Baptist Church area is geographically triangular between Inkberry Road and Tabernacle Road boarding Hwy 394 out of Salley, South Carolina. The church, formerly known as Chapman Baptist Church, is presently Harvest of Love Outreach Ministries.

[38] Ibid.

[39] Death Certificate for George Piper, 13 March 1921, File No. 18351, State of South Carolina, Bureau of Vital Statistics, State Board of Heath, www.ancestry.com.

[40] General Sessions Court Convened, Aiken, South Carolina, Aiken Standard, 28 September 1921, p.1, www.newspapers.com.

defense attorneys.[41] There was array of witnesses who gave testimony, and the case went over into the next day.[42]

Because Governor had good relations with local Whites in the community, it worked to his advantage. He was able to post bond.[43] In doing so, it incited anger among many of Piper's friends because they felt Governor should remained in custody.[44] One of Piper's friends named John "Rack" Odom, was plotting to murder Governor to avenge Piper's death.[45] On the last week of June 1921, Governor had just come home from Mr. Brodie store, and seated himself at the dining table with his family.[46] While were eating supper, his son Governor "Mint" Thompson, Jr. was sitting with his back to the window in the dining room, and Governor facing the window across table from his son. About the time Governor took his seat, Odom who rode a mule buggy to Governor's home wearing a pair of woman's shoes, sneaked up to the house and fired shots through a small crack in the window severely wounded Governor's son Mint. Mint died shortly after.[47] [48]

Then the Sheriff along with several neighbors investigated the cause of the incident. At first, no hint of the murderer was given, but the women's shoe track led in a circuitous route from some distance to a road where it ended by the murderer entering a waiting buggy.[49] The track of the mule hitched to the vehicle was then taken up; the shoes found in Governor's home, and gradually the circumstantial

---

[41] General Sessions Court Convened, p.1.

[42] Ibid.

[43] Attempted Murder at Kitchings Mill, Aiken, South Carolina, The Journal and Review, 29 June 1921, p.1, www.newspapers.com.

[44] Attempted Murder at Kitchings Mill, p.1

[45] Aiken County News Notes, Aiken, South Carolina, The Journal and Review, 6 July 1921, p.8, www.newspapers.com.

[46] Ibid.

[47] "Rack" Odom Gets Life Sentence for Killing Colored Boy-Fallaw Must Open Road, Aiken, South Carolina, The Journal and Review, 12 October 1921, p.1, www.newspapers.com.

[48] Boys Dies Of Wounds, Aiken, South Carolina, The Journal and Review, 6 July 1921, p.8, www.newspapers.com.

[49] "Rack" Odom Gets Life Sentence for Killing Colored Boy-Fallaw Must Open Road, p.1.

evidence would firm around John Odom.[50] The evidence also showed that the murderer was trying to kill Governor and not his son. The Skillet and the surrounding communities were wrought over the attempted assassination. They feared that the assailant would not hesitate to attack anyone who he had a grievance against.

On June 28, 1921, Odom was arrested and charged for the murder of young Mint. The trial lasted for two days. There were twenty-nine witnesses for the State and fourteen for the defense was sworn in. The Hon. John F. Williams assisted the solicitor and W.M. Smoak, Esq. acted for the defense. People on the jury were H.C. Weeks, foreman; Claude Cumbee, J.O. Lybrand, G.W. Plunkett, B.K. Boylston, B.G. Hall, T.W. Cummings, R.L. Holsonbake, Lewis Adams, J.E. Bryan, George Solomon, and T.T. Derrick. The jury rendered a guilty verdict and sentenced Odom to life in prison.

After the tragedy, Governor and his family moved to Washington, District of Columbia. He died on February 14, 1944, at the age of 60.[51] Later, Governor wife Sustanchia moved back to South Carolina and resided in Aiken. She died on September 19, 1957, at the age of 63.[52] They are both buried at Smyrna Missionary Baptist Church.

---

[50] Ibid.

[51] Death Certificate for Governor Logan Thompson, Jr., 28 June 1921, File No. 18352, State of South Carolina, Bureau of Vital Statistics, State Board of Heath, www.ancestry.com.

[52] Death Certificate for Sustanchia Thompson, 19 September 1957, File No. 12947, State of South Carolina, Bureau of Vital Statistics, State Board of Heath, www.ancestry.com.

The Self-Identity Crisis and Redemption of Joseph Pitts Thompson

By Cloté Zettie Gantt Davis, RN, MN, Ph.D., granddaughter

During my early childhood, my mother, Ruth Pitts Thompson Gantt, begun to share her family history with me as she performed her household chores, i.e., washing clothes, cooking meals, etc. The details I am about to share with you, may not be completely historically correct, but it is as I remember.

Mom stated her mother Rivanna Corley-Thompson died when she was two (2) weeks old and she was cared for by her dad, Joseph Thompson, and her older siblings. At the age of five (5) years old, she clearly remembered one night her father hitched up a mule to a wagon, took a few items of furniture and a lover and hastily left town. He had a cow tied to the back of the wagon. This departure took place in the small community of Salley, South Carolina. The reason for Joseph leaving in the dark of night was important—His lover was a white female and in 1909 this act would have gotten him killed, had he been caught.

Allow me to interject here the history of my grandfather's birth. His mother, Amanda Friday, was working in the kitchen of the slave owner of the plantation where he was born.[53] As custom during that day, the slave masters often fathered children by the house slaves, therefore Joseph was born the son of the white master and the slave cook in the kitchen. His first years were spent in slavery. His complexion was more like his father than his mother, and that is why he could leave town with a white lady and not be killed once he left Salley.

My mom grew up, got married, and moved to Washington, DC, were she continuously searched for her father through radio

---

[53] Joseph Pitts Thompson mother named is Amanda Friday, who later married Milledge Thompson, his stepfather. Therefore, he adopted "Thompson" as his last name.

17

announcements, etc. In later years he told her, when he returned home, that he was working in Savannah, GA at a filling station, heard the announcement that Ruth Thompson was looking for Joseph Thompson. Then he went inside, collected his pay, and moved to Stone Mountain, Georgia. This is when he assumed the name Pitts, his father's name, the slave owner.

As I was about six (6) years old, I remember my uncle Philip Thompson bringing a letter to my mom and telling her that the letter was from their father, she stopped cooking and began to read it aloud. I listened intently, and this is what I heard. "This is your father Joseph Thompson writing for you children to come to Stone Mountain, GA and get me, I am an old man now and I want to come home."

The very next morning, my mom and two (2) of her sisters were on their way to Stone Mountain, GA and a few days later they returned with a little man that all the siblings remembered as dad. He lived with his children for three (3) years until he passed in 1949 and is buried at Zion Hill Missionary Baptist Church, Wagener, SC.[54] According to him, his age at death was 93, his birth date on his head stone is not what he always stated.

---

[54] Death Certificate for Joseph Thompson, 20 February 1949, File No. C1114, State of South Carolina, Bureau of Vital Statistics, State Board of Heath, www.ancestry.com.

Phillip Thompson: From Sharecropper to Soil Conservationist

Phillip Thompson was one of seven children born to Joseph and Rivanna Corley Thompson on February 15, 1895, in the Kitchings Mill Community outside of Salley, South Carolina. At an early age, he joined Oakey Springs Missionary Baptist Church near Springfield, South Carolina. Later, he married Inez Thompson. Out of their union, two daughters were born: Gladys Gilbert and Gloria Nichols.

During the old days, some southern sharecroppers desired financial independence purchased land for themselves and their families. Phillip was one of them. He purchased 95 acres in the Salley area and embarked on an illustrious career in soil conservation. He cultivated many inventive ways to conserve soil that garnered local recognition. On February 10, 1943, Phillip along with several African American farmers to receive an award of merit competing in the Aiken County Better Farm Living Program contest in producing 75% of their farm needs in food and feed.[55] [56]

Local newspapers frequently observed Phillip practices and highlighted his work, chronologized accordingly:

- March 12, 1943, the Aiken Standard and Review reported Phillip efforts in planting Kobe Lespedeza on his property and quoted him for complementing the Edisto Soil Conservation District for loaning him two horses to construct "T" terraces.[57]

- June 30, 1943, the Aiken Standard highlighted Phillip boasting about educating his hogs to eat Kobe lespedeza for soil conservation purposes.[58]

---

[55] Aiken Farmers Receive Awards of Merit for '42, Aiken, South Carolina, Aiken Standard and Review, 10 February 1943, p.1 and p.3, www.newspapers.com.

[56] Chris Thompson, 1st Cousin of Phillip Thompson, also received an award of merit competing in the Aiken County Better Farm Living Program contest. Ibid, Aiken Farmers Receive Awards of Merit for '42.

[57] County and Home Agents Discuss Advantages of Victory Gardens, Aiken, South Carolina, Aiken Standard and Review, 12 March 1943, p.2, www.newspapers.com.

[58] Colored News By Home and Farm Agents, Aiken, South Carolina, Aiken Standard, 30 June 1943, p.8, www.newspapers.com.

- January 10, 1945, the Aiken Standard reported that Phillip prepped three acres on his farm to grow sericea as a "labor saver" to reduce the burden of plowing land for hay to advert attention to other labor needs on the farm.[59]

On April 28, 1952, Phillip, along with several local black farmers, Otis McCloud, Donald Quattlebaum (grandson of Isaac and Charlotte Thompson-Quattlebaum), and Julia S. Woodward, signed a Cooperative Agreement with the Aiken Soil Conservation District to use their land as a "field site" to test terrace maintenance techniques.[60] On their farms, about eight miles of terraces were constructed to help hold the soil in place.[61] Outlets into the woods for the terraces were constructed and where needed, special waterways were made to carry off the excess water.[62] The waterways and field boarders on their farms planted sericea for erosion control.

Phillip died on August 17, 1956, at the age of 62. Phillip is buried at Oakey Springs Missionary Baptist Church.[63]

---

[59] The Colony, Aiken, South Carolina, Aiken Standard, 10 January 1945, p.8, www.newspapers.com.

[60] Farming Practices Paying Off, Aiken, South Carolina, The Journal and Review, 28 April 1952, p.2, www.newspapers.com.

[61] Farming Practices Paying Off, p.2

[62] Ibid.

[63] Death Certificate for Phillip Thompson, 17 August 1956, File No. 009771, State of South Carolina, Bureau of Vital Statistics, State Board of Heath, www.ancestry.com.

Isaac and Charlotte Quattlebaum: Former Slaves Who Lived Victoriously

Excerpts from "Roots" The 1987 Quattlebaum Family Reunion book

Isaac Quattlebaum, better known as "Grandpa", was born a slave on March 15, 1844, near Saluda, South Carolina.[64] At the age of five, his mother Molly was sold and left him trying to hold on to her apron string. With her son crying and trying to cling to his mother, she was sold anyway without any compassion for the affections between she and her son. While little known of Isaac's family, he had two sisters and one brother. His wife, Charlotte Thompson-Quattlebaum, better known as "Grandma", the daughter of Milledge and Laura Thompson, was also a slave born in 1846 in Charleston, South Carolina.[65] Like Isaac, her mother was also sold. Later in Charlotte's life, her father was able to both secure her and her sister Clara Thompson-Livingston their freedom. She had 16 siblings: ten brothers, 5 sisters, and one stepbrother.

Isaac and Charlotte were married around 1860, when Isaac was 16 years old, and Charlotte was 14 years old. Out of their union, fourteen children were born: Maggie Quattlebaum-Johnson, Alice Quattlebaum, Harvey Quattlebaum, Milledge Quattlebaum (name after Charlotte's father, Milledge), Selena Quattlebaum-Stevens, George Quattlebaum, Alex Quattlebaum, Pollie Quattlebaum-Taylor (name after Charlotte's half-sister, Pollie), Boliver Quattlebaum, Luther Quattlebaum, Laura Quattlebaum Daniels-Grant, John Quattlebaum, and Murray Quattlebaum. They had opposite personalities complemented each other which provided the balance that kept their marriage solid. Isaac was characterized as a patient, mild-mannered Christian gentleman who was loved and respected by all who

---

[64] Birth Certificate for John W. Quattlebaum, 12 October 1942, South Carolina Delayed Birth Records (1766-1900) and City of Charleston, South Carolina Birth Records (1877-1901), www.ancestry.com.

[65] Birth Certificate for John W. Quattlebaum.

encountered him which is quite noteworthy considering this was during slavery and post slavery years. He attended church on a regular basis, taking his family along also. Isaac was one of the first deacons at Smyrna Missionary Baptist Church and was well acquainted with the ministers of the church whom he and Charlotte often entertained in their home. Charlotte was a Christian also, but hardly the mild mannered individual that her husband was. She was highly emotional and spirited with a fiery temper. Despite this, Charlotte was a good wife and mother. Because Charlotte was so young when she married Isaac, Isaac had to teach her everything especially about cooking. As a result, she became an excellent cook.

Isaac was a farmer and entrepreneur. He and Charlotte brought 90 acres of land on which had a syrup mill and on which they built their home.[66] Unfortunately, the house wasn't built until after all the children were grown. The children were raised on rented property where Isaac farmed before he purchased his land. In fact, by farming this land and saving his money, he was able to purchase the 90 acres. In those days, cash was not easily accessible, so Isaac, being the compassionate person that he was, sometimes accepted jugs of syrup from his customers at the mill instead of money. Family was also important to Isaac. On every July 4, he would barbeque pork and hold a family reunion with all his children and grandchildren.

Isaac died at home in March of 1922 at the ripe old age of 83, and Charlotte died on January 19, 1940, at the remarkable age of 94.[67] [68] They are both buried next to each other at Smyrna Missionary Baptist Church.

---

[66] Deed of Sale from Claudia Brodie et.al to Isaac Quattlebaum and Harvey Quattlebaum, 23 February 1901 (recorded 17 June 1901), Deed Book 11-1, page 215, Aiken County Grantee Index Conveyance Book, O-Z, South Carolina Department of Archives and History.

[67] Death Certificate for Isaac Quattlebaum, March 1922, File No. 4725, State of South Carolina, Bureau of Vital Statistics, State Board of Heath, www.ancestry.com.

[68] Death Certificate for Charlotte Quattlebaum, 19 January 1940, File No. 1810, State of South Carolina, Bureau of Vital Statistics, State Board of Heath, www.ancestry.com.

Lavinia Corley Thompson: South Carolina African American Female Confederate Veteran

The Middle Passage was the stage of the triangular trade in which millions of Africans were shipped to the "New World" as part of the Atlantic slave trade. Millions of Africans were captured and sold as slave labor in Europe, North America, and South America. Infamously, the Middle Passage is widely known historically as one of the most barbaric events that involved genocidal monstrosity of African people. Africans were brutally treated like savages experiencing trauma and malnutrition. They were chained together on large ships during the long gruesome voyage to their respective destinations. Those who were physically impaired or had infirmities were killed instantly; and some were thrown off the ship, prey for sharks who regularly followed the ships feasting off disposed bodies. During the Middle Passage, an enslaved African woman named Phyliss Corley sojourned to the shores of South Carolina.[69] She was later purchased by the Corley family who lived near Kitchings Mill located in the Barnwell District.[70] Phyliss later had a courting relationship with a man named Robert Staley. Out of their union, Lavinia was born on June 3, 1844.[71] [72] She was a slave of Samuel G. Webb, who married his daughter, Charlotte Corley.[73]

---

[69] Thompson Family Reunion Book published on July 1987.

[70] It is inferred that Phyliss Corley was purchased by Joshua Corley, who was the father of Charlotte Corley-Webb and father-in-law of Samuel G. Webb, who were Lavinia slave masters. Therefore, Phyliss last name is "Corley".

[71] Lavinia had many surnames. "Viney", "Levinie", and "Elviny".

[72] Death Certificate for Levinie Thompson, 8 June 1928, File No. 9632, State of South Carolina, Bureau of Vital Statistics, State Board of Heath.

[73] 1860; U.S. Federal Census Place-Slave Schedules: Washington, D.C; National Archives and Records Administration, 1860. M653, 1,438 rolls. Ancestry.com, assessed June 10, 2018, www.ancestry.com.

[93] Ibid, Thompson Family Reunion Book.

Lavinia's granddaughter, Nettie Thompson-Johnson (daughter of Oscar J. and Lessie Thompson), shared an oral account that Lavinia shared with her and other grandchildren. The account is documented in the old Thompson Family Reunion book.[74]

> Viney Corley Thompson is the wife of Reverend Logan Thompson. Mary Woodward Evans is the wife of Daniel Evans. Both were born to a slave mother from Africa, who was brought here on a boat. The morning Viney (as she was called) and Mary were going to be sold in Tallahassee, Florida the two girls talked it over and each said they were going to listen real good to here and see where they were being sold to and to whom. But we do know that Viney was sold for $100.00. Grandma Viney later told her story to some of her grandchildren (Nettie Thompson Johnson, uncle Oscar's daughter) Grandma Viney said "I must have been the pretty thing that day because I bought in that much money". She told the slave auctioneer "You might as well sell me over because I ain't a go'." At the time her dress was white. Her master beat her all the way home 'till her dress was so bloody that you couldn't see the white on it. Later in life Viney and Mary found each other. Sometimes later Viney's granddaughter, Nettie Johnson would be in church and see this lady at Smyrna Baptist Church in Salley, S.C. and thought it was grandma Viney. It was Viney's sister Mary W. Evans. Both were very strong women and lived to be very old grandmothers.

On December 20, 1860, thirteen states took a leap of faith to declare their freedom to govern themselves which led to the formation of the Confederate States of America. Samuel declared his allegiance to the Confederacy, enlisted in the 11th Regiment Reserves, making up the 1st Corps of South Carolina Reserves, as a private.[75] He served in Company A, from Barnwell, commanded by Joseph Stallings. The regiment served from November 11, 1862, to February 16, 1863, later conscripted to the Department of South Carolina, Georgia, and Florida for its entire existence.[76] Then, on September 1, 1863, Lavinia joined Samuel serving as a cook under his authority until the end of the war.[77]

During the war, both Samuel and Lavinia were amid combative and non-combative environments, chronologized accordingly:[78]

- From September 22, 1863, until May or June 1864, Samuel was employed at the Augusta Arsenal located in Augusta, Georgia: a facility that produced enormous quantities of military technology for the Confederate Army.[79] [80]

- November 15, 1864, Samuel was conscripted into Company A, 15th Lucas Battalion, South Carolina Heavy Artillery in Columbia, South Carolina. Company A was based at Battery Pringle along the Stono River on James Island, near Charleston, South Carolina.[81] [82]

- In early 1865, the 15th Lucas Battalion, was converted to infantry. The battalion was under Rhett Brigade, which

---

[75] Pension application for Lavinia Thompson, Records of the Comptroller General, Pension Applications, 1919-1926, #496. South Carolina Department of Archives and History.

[76] Seigler, Robert S., *South Carolina's military organizations during the War between the States.* Charleston: History Press, 2008.

[77] Pension application for Lavinia Thompson.

[78] Although Lavinia served as cook under Samuel G. Webb throughout the war, it was possible that she was with Samuel in combative and non-combative environments.

[79] Seigler, Robert S., *South Carolina's military organizations during the War between the States.*

[80] "Civil War Service Records, Confederate Records," digital images, Fold3, 1st Local Troops Infantry, pg. 1-5, entry for Samuel G. Webb, www.Fold3.com.

[81] "Civil War Service Records", pg. 1-5.

[82] "Civil War Service Records, Confederate Records," digital images, Fold3, Fifteenth (Lucas') Battalion, pg. 1-4, entry for S.G.B Webb, www.Fold3.com.

functioned as the rear guard during the Confederate withdrawal into North Carolina in February and March 1865.[83]

After the war ended in 1865, Lavinia met and married the Rev. Logan Thompson in 1871.[84] Out of their union, 6 children were born: Della Thompson-Rowe, Governor Thompson, Robert Thompson, Queen Thompson-Corley, Effie Thompson Simmons, and Oscar J. Thompson. In addition, Logan had seven children from a previous marriage: Lydia Thompson-Kitchings, Dora Thompson, Willie Thompson, Corey Thompson, Rosanna Thompson-Rice, Elizabeth Thompson, and Denna Thompson.[85] The family lived in the Skillet community and attended Smyrna Missionary Baptist Church. Occupationally, Logan was a carpenter/farmer and Lavinia was a housekeeper. When Logan died on August 4, 1901, the day before his birthday, Lavinia became a widower living next door to her children.

On March 16, 1923, the South Carolina Legislature approved pensions to African Americans who faithfully served in the Confederate Army. Known as Act 63, the law stipulated that African Americans who served in the Confederacy as servants, cooks, or attendants were eligible for a pension.[86] Other qualifications included at least six months of active service, recommendation of the County Pension Board, and supporting affidavits.[87] Lavinia, who served until the end of the war, applied for her pension on May 11, 1923.[88] Three days later, her pension was approved on May 15, 1923.

---

[83] "Civil War Service Records, pg. 1-4.

[84] Logan Thompson was born on August 5, 1832.

[85] Logan first wife was Cornelia Thompson.

[86] Helsley, Jones Alexia, *South Carolina's African American Confederate Pensioners 1923-1925*. South Carolina Department of Archives and History, 1998.

[87] Helsely, Jones Alexia, *South Carolina's African American Confederate Pensioners 1923-1925*.

[88] Ibid.

On June 8, 1928, three days after her birthday, Lavinia died as a widow at the ripe old age of 84. Lavinia is buried next to her husband, Logan, at Smyrna Missionary Baptist Church.[89]

---

[89] Death Certificate for Levinie Thompson.

Oscar J. Thompson, Sr.: From Sharecropper to Entrepreneur

Oscar J. Thompson, Sr., was one of five children born to the Rev. Logan L. and Lavinia Corley-Thompson on March 5, 1881, in the Skillet community outside of Salley, South Carolina. At an early age, he joined Smyrna Missionary Baptist Church where he was ordained as a deacon.

Like his parents, Oscar was a sharecropper. Briefly, he lived with his brother Robert Thompson and his family until he was able to support himself. Later, he married Lessie Felder. Out their union, twelve children were born: Oscar Thompson, Jr., Austin Thompson, Warren Harding Thompson, Osban Thompson, Jerome Thompson, Eddie Lee Thompson, Nettie Thompson-Johnson, Lena Thompson-Lloyd, Mamie Thompson-Shuler, Carrie Thompson Morgan-Horne, and Dorothy Thompson Dumas-Parks, and an adopted son, Paul Goodwin.[90] In addition, Oscar had two children, Alice Thompson-Seawright and Balem Thompson, Sr., from previous relationships.[91]

Oscar and his family continued to sharecrop for several years. While working, he saved his money with the goal of becoming a landowner. On December 9, 1915, Oscar purchased 92 acres from David Link of Deland, Florida; on October 4, 1916, Oscar purchased 96 acres from Bertie Rice, a relative of his brother-in-law, Jacob Rice, who married his half-sister Rosanna Thompson-Rice for $100; and on

---

[90] Oscar and Lessie had two infant sons who died prematurely. One died on October 15, 1911 and other died on July 20, 1913. They are both buried at Smyrna Baptist Church, Springfield, South Carolina.

[91] In-person conversation with Catherine Seawright-McCollough, daughter of Robert Lee and Alice Thompson-Seawright, 1996, by Walter B. Curry, Jr., at Catherine's home in Salley, South Carolina.

December 23, 1919, he purchased an additional 42 acres from Viana Corbett, Susie Johnson, and Reanna Martin for $1,300.[92] [93] [94]

Oscar was full-fledged entrepreneur. In agriculture, he cultivated his farm into a full-scale operation that garnered local acclaim. The local newspaper lauded his three-year crop rotation system.[95] To further his knowledge in agriculture, Oscar joined a group of local African American farmers on a field trip to Coker Pedigreed Farm in Hartsville, South Carolina "to study and observe seed breeding and other farm practices." [96] [97] In real estate, he sold property to his relatives. On August 12, 1918, he sold 22 acres of land to his first cousin, James "Vet" Thompson wife, Keller Thompson for $200.00; and sold 42 acres to his wife parents, Henry and Eliza Felder for $775.00.[98] [99] [100]

---

[92] Deed of Sale from David Link to Oscar Thompson, 9 December 1915 (recorded 18 January 1916), Deed Book 25, page 172, Aiken County Grantee Index Conveyance Book, O-Z, South Carolina Department of Archives and History.

[93] Deed of Sale from Bertie Rice to Oscar Thompson, 4 October 1916 (recorded 29 November 1916) Deed Book 26, page 307, Aiken County Grantee Index Conveyance Book, O-Z, South Carolina Department of Archives and History.

[94] Deed of Sale from Vianna Corbett et.al to Oscar Thompson, 23 December 1919 (recorded 24 December 1919) Deed Book 34, page 119, Aiken County Grantee Index Conveyance Book, O-Z, South Carolina Department of Archives and History.

[95] Soil Conservation, Aiken, South Carolina, The Journal and Review, 17 February 1943, p.2, www.newspapers.com.

[96] Negro Farmers Visit Coker Seed Plant, Aiken Standard and Review, Aiken, South Carolina, 9 August 1944, p.8, www.newspapers.com.

[97] Coker Seed Plant, a subsidiary company of Coker Experimental Farms, founded by David Coker in the early 1900's. The company developed new, innovative varieties of crop seeds which included the first cotton breeding program in the U.S. Today, Coker Farms is a national historic landmark, www.discoversouthcarolina.com/products/25739.

[98] James "Vet" Thompson is the son of Anderson and Anna Livingston-Thompson.

[99] Deed of Sale from Oscar Thompson to Keller Thompson, 12 August 1918 (recorded 15 August 1918) Deed Book 29, page 334, Aiken County Grantee Index Conveyance Book, O-Z, South Carolina Department of Archives and History.

[100] Real Estate Transfers, Aiken, South Carolina, The Journal and Review, 17 October 1943, p.3, www.newspapers.com.

Oscar died on August 11, 1945, at the age of 64.[101] Four years later, his wife Lessie died on September 21, 1949, at the age of 56.[102] They are both buried next to each other at Smyrna Missionary Baptist Church.

---

[101] Death Certificate for Oscar J. Thompson, 11 August 1945, File No. 08484, State of South Carolina, Bureau of Vital Statistics, State Board of Heath, www.ancestry.com.
[102] Death Certificate for Lessie Thompson, 21 September 1949, File No. 013591

Joshua and Queen Thompson-Corley: Symbolic Figures of Grittiness

By Toretha Corley-Wright, granddaughter

> Merriam-Webster defines grittiness as the strength of mind that enables a person to endure pain or hardship.

Born on Thanksgiving Day, 1880, about 15 years after the signing of the Emancipation Proclamation by President Abraham Lincoln, Joshua Corley just did escape the ordeal of slavery. Still the fourth child born to ex-slaves would be a sharecropper working the fertile soil in the South Carolina County of Aiken. There would be no school for poor children like Josh. They would be consigned to help in the fields planting or harvesting throughout the year.

Josh was a quiet and caring young man who worked long hours in the cotton fields to help feed his family. It said that he would work so long in the cotton fields that at the end of the day his finger would be blood red from picking the cotton fiber from those cotton bolls. But no one in the fields could fill up a sack of cotton as fast as he could. He was a young man in his twenties before he met and married the woman with whom he would spend the rest of his life. Queen Thompson was born on Christmas Eve in 1886, the fourth child born to Logan Thompson (b. 1832) and Levine Corley Thompson (b. 1844) both former slaves. A strong-willed, but happy young woman from the same part of the county, known for saying what she meant and meaning what she said, captured Josh's heart and that was that. It is unclear how they first met, but we can be certain that once they got together, it was forever. That union produced twelve children: Julian (b. 1904) Laura, who died of fever at age 6 (b. 1908); Robert (b. 1909); Fred (b. 1910); Frank (b. 1912); Sherman (b. 1914); Phillip (b. 1916); Ella Mae (b. 1918); Joshua Jr. (b. 1920); Henry (b. 1922); George (b. 1924); and Victoria (b. 1926).

Although they lived during the Depression Era, if you had asked any one of them how the depression affected them, they would

31

ask, "What Depression?" And that was the attitude of the family. They had very little material wealth, but they were rich with love and kindheartedness.

During their years of farming, the family sharecropped for white farm owner, Benny Cumbee, "a good white lady", by the name of Anna Hutto, Theodore Weeks in Montmorenci, Ben Williams of Hitchcock Farms also known as Cedar Grove, and Harold Cullum. Queen made sure her family would get food to eat whether the year produced a good crop of peas, beans, and corn or not. It was her contention that they worked hard all season; it was up to the good Lord to provide the bounty. If He saw fit to send a small crop that was no reason for her family to suffer.

One season when the gathering of the harvest was less than expected, the wealthy farm owner came in his big truck to get his fair share. Because of the thinness of the crop that year, the farm owner wanted "more than his fair share." It is our understanding that Queen said her children had to eat and gave the man such a severe tongue-lashing that he left with his tail between his legs and never made such a foolish request again.

Josh was a deacon at Cedar Grove Baptist Church, Aiken, while Queen retained her membership at Smyrna Missionary Baptist Church, the Thompson family church. During their farming on the Hitchcock Farm, the family attended Mt. Anna Baptist Church. Josh, Queen, and some of their children (Josh, Jr., Philip, and Victoria) are buried in the Smyrna Baptist Church Cemetery.

Other stories I heard from older cousins Henry (John Henry Winfield) and Tweet (John Corley) were about her cooking. According to them, she made the best sorghum biscuits they ever tasted then and now.

Josh died in 1950. Two years later, Queen died on January 17, 1952. They are both buried in the Smyrna Missionary Baptist Church cemetery.

NARRATIVE ANALYSES

I. From "Milledge Thompson: A Freedman's Story"

Milledge Thompson was one of the many former slaves who were able to obtain their freedom. It is not known on how he was able to obtain his freedom, but what is known that an opportunity was afforded to him to obtain it. What is quite remarkable was the generosity of local Whites who helped obtain Milledge's freedom. Their efforts could have attested to Milledge's character.

Milledge, like other freedmen, secured the freedom of their families. He was quite aware of the malevolent realities of slavery in the practice of separating enslaved families. Although his first wife Laura was sold without remorse; remarkably, he secured the freedom of his two oldest children, Charlotte, and Clara. For several years, he raised them as a single father; at the same time vigilant because of the pervasive marginalization of freedmen during the Antebellum period Freedmen rights and movements in South Carolina were legally restricted. Even the threat of enslavement was a frightening reality for many freedmen like Milledge.

Milledge faced the burden of being a devoted husband. Amanda, Milledge's second wife, had a goiter on the right of her neck, that limited her movements along with the infirmities. Secondly, she had a child, Joseph Pitts Thompson, from her slave master. The nature of her relationship with the slave master is unknown, but if she was violated or assaulted, no doubt she experienced psychological trauma. More than likely, Milledge was aware of those issues.

Milledge also dealt with the animosity between his wife Amanda and his daughter Charlotte for reasons unknown. Both were strong-willed women who weren't far apart in age. Nevertheless, it deeply concerned Milledge. Knowing the magnitude of the situation, he took it upon himself to introduce Charlotte to his children. It was that moment, the impasse between Charlotte and Amanda was broken.

Milledge desire for self-independence culminated in purchasing land, acquiring 100 acres for $2.00 acre. Unfortunately, after his death and later his wife, their children were unable to keep the land because of two reasons: infighting among themselves and better economic opportunities elsewhere. If the land was kept, his descendants could have use it as an asset to create wealth. This mistake had punitive consequences that affected family relations both socially and economically for many years. A mistake, corollary of the conundrum concerning the significant loss of heir properties among African American families in the rural South, especially South Carolina.

Milledge was one the first ordained deacons at Smyrna Baptist Church. In the church's early years, his descendants led the church through difficult and convivial times. They served and continually serving as deacons, trustees, and other positions within the church. Other descendants have served and currently serving in leadership roles at local and non-local churches. Many people were and still are directly impacted by the ministerial work of Milledge's descendants.

II. From "Otis Thompson, Sr.: An Individual With Many Vocations"

Otis Thompson, Sr. truly was a man with many vocations. His versatility in his vocations was quite remarkable. He chose to live an active life of full vibrancy, not settling for dullness. Furthermore, Otis was not defined to a monistic vocation, but his vocations were pluralistic and meaningful.

His involvement in the fundraising effort to help rebuild Piney Grove school is significant. Piney Grove school was one of many African American schools throughout the rural South Carolina specifically Aiken County during the Jim Crow era. Many of them faced daunting challenges because poor funding and curriculum inequalities. As a result, African Americans took upon themselves to support their own schools. Their support was necessary for African American children to receive an education most of the time in substandard conditions and pernicious circumstances. Otis's involvement demonstrated his support for quality education among African-American children in the Skillet Community; furthermore, Otis occupation as a farmer had no bearing in his advocacy. With little formal education, he recognized the imperativeness of civic engagement as an impetus. During the Jim Crow era, civic engagement was pervasive among many African Americans era regardless of individual occupation, to support African American schools. Collective self-determination was the driving force; the same force that could be instrumental to strengthen and empower public and private schools with predominant African American students. Otis, members of Smyrna Baptist Church, and the local community recognized that the reemergence of Piney Grove school was not just the sole responsibility of government, but their own collective responsibility induced with collective self-determination.

During the Great Depression (1929-1933), the United States suffered a severe economic depression that resulted in widespread poverty and depravity. African Americans who were already economically periled suffered the most, specifically farmers who owned land. Many African Americans were forced to sell their land due to the scarcity of economic opportunities. Very aware of the threat, Otis temporarily moved his family to Washington, DC securing employment to save his farm and his family. This sacrifice resulted in keeping the farm until it was sold in the early 1940's.

Otis involvement in the timber industry is very insightful. There is minimal discourse in the African American community about the benefits of forestry as an economic utility. Yet Otis recognized the meaning and importance of sustainable forestry as an imperative strategy to cultivate the land. Selling timber for $650 in 1941 went a long way especially in conundrum system of Jim Crow, and the monstrosity of the Great Depression that adversely affected the quality of life of many African Americans. Otis foresight recognized this reality. Given the history of persistent wealth inequality among African Americans, it would be wise to consider forestry as an integral part of future constructive, wealth building efforts, especially individuals and families who are landowners.

III. From "The Vigilante Exploits of Murry Quattlebaum"

The conventional wisdom among southern African Americans during the Jim Crow era was avoid confrontation with southern Whites. Some African Americans knew that confronting Whites, especially Whites who had political influence, was very risky. Under those circumstances, African Americans had to walk a "tight line" in their relations with Whites.

As an African American man, Murry was very aware of the dangerous risk in confronting Chief Luke Rodgers, a White man. He was quite knowledgeable of the law when he asked Chief Rodgers and his accomplice Constable Norris Johnson to show the warrant to arrest his brother. Then, Murry shot Chief Rodgers. He justified his action out of fear claiming that Chief Rodgers was shooting at him.

The most striking finding is that Murry was able to post bail without serving prison time. Due to the nature of the crime, Murray was supposed to be severely punished. This never happened because of his relationship with Dr. Brodie, a prominent local White male doctor. While many African Americans were denied legal rights during the Jim Crow era, an argument could be made that some African Americans were exonerated from crimes because of their harmonious relationships with prominent Whites, evident in Murry's situation.

IV. From "Tragedy in the Skillet: The Murder of Young Governor "Mint" Thompson, Jr".

The beginning of this tragedy started when George Piper was intoxicated with alcohol. Learning from the experiences senior family relatives who lived during rural South, African Americans drunk alcohol recreationally and therapeutically. Farmers who toil long hours in the fields drunk alcohol for relaxation. On the weekends, alcohol was a frequent beverage at social gatherings. The perils of

36

sharecropping and racial discrimination adversely affected some African Americans to the point that some drank alcohol as a temporary mental escape.

Understanding the above exposition gives a contextual view the mental disposition of Piper. What was going on with him that he became wildly intoxicated? Unfortunately, Piper left behind his wife and children. If Piper had self-temperance, he would have lived. During slavery and the post-slavery era, temperance and abstinence was encouraged by many African American leaders and African American churches to mitigate the negative effects of alcohol; so, tragedies like Piper could be adverted. Later, other civic and religious organizations encouraged African Americans to embrace sobriety and abstain from alcohol.

Piper erratic behavior from his drunkenness alarmed his friend, Governor H. Thompson, Sr. Although Governor murdered Piper in self-defense, the negative effect of alcohol has punitive consequences ranging resulting in negative behavior, criminal activity, etc. Sadly, how quickly friends turn into enemies when alcohol usage is perverted. Governor had to suffer silently in grief knowing he had taken a friend life.

Governor was arrested and charged with murder. During the Jim Crow era, African Americans faced obstacles in obtaining quality legal representation, but it was unusual for an African American like Governor to obtain legal representation and post bond to obtain his freedom. His positive relationships with local Whites aided in his defense.

While Governor enjoyed his freedom, several of Piper's friends were indignant because they felt Governor should have been denied bond. Obvious of their indignation was towards Governor, but could there been other motives? Were they upset because Governor had close ties to local Whites? Piper's friends could have contemplated these questions.

One of Piper's friend, John "Rack" Odom decided to take the "law" in his own hands by murdering Governor to avenged Piper's death. Although, he came close in shooting Governor, he tragically shot Governor's son "Mint" who died from the gunshot wound. Remorseful, Odom was arrested, convicted, and received a life sentence in prison. Odom suffered silently in grief knowing that he murdered an innocent little boy.

V. From "The Self Identity Crisis and Redemption of Joseph Pitts Thompson"

Born of an enslaved mother whose father was a White slaveowner, Joseph Pitts Thompson lived during the time W.E.B Dubois (1903) declared, "The problem of the Twentieth Century is the problem of the color-line" (3).[103] The color line that is, centered on the centrality of race in the phenomena of American culture and life throughout the Twentieth Century. Race was one of many primary factors that determined social, economic, and political mobility. It shaped cultural norms, behaviors, attitudes, public policy, religion, education, etc.

As a mulatto, Joseph was very aware of the color line. The color line determined cultural norms and beliefs of straight courting. During the Jim Crow era in the rural South, sexual racism was very much alive. Most Whites and African Americans discouraged interracial relationships out of fear and disruption of the social order. If an African American man was seen with a White woman, it was perceived as an abomination. African American men risked being tortured or killed if they were caught courting White women.

Knowing the threat, Joseph and his White lover left Salley, South Carolina. Although, sexual racism was a primary reason, but what other reasons compelled Joseph to leave? Was it the death of his wife, Rivanna? Was it the uncertainty of rearing his children as a single parent? Was he ridiculed because he was a mulatto by local Whites and

---

[103] Du Bois, W. E. B. (1903). *The Souls of Black Folk*. New York: Barnes & Noble Classic, p.3.

African Americans? Whatever reason, he left his family behind to fend for themselves.

When Joseph was living in Savannah, Georgia, he heard the radio announcement that his daughter Ruth was looking for him. Frightened, Joseph left Savannah, changed his last name to "Pitts" (last name of his father) and moved to Stone Mountain, Georgia with his father's family. While living there, he experienced a self-epiphany. He wrote a letter to his children asking them to bring him home. Ruth along with sisters' children obliged.

This narrative depicts the self-identity crisis that Joseph experienced during his life. The psychological trauma caused by sexual racism coupled with the loss of his wife could have been too much for him to manage. Consequently, for many years, he was an absentee father. Yet he redeemed himself by acknowledging that he needed to come home and make amends with his children.

I wonder what Ruth and her sisters were thinking on the ride to Stone Mountain to pick up their father. They could have resented him for all the years he was absent from their lives, but they forgave him. Their forgiveness was instrumental for Joseph in his redemption. No longer bound by the self-identity crisis, he lived the last few years of his life with his family.

VI. From "Phillip Thompson: From Sharecropper to Soil Conservationist"

During his childhood, Phillip Thompson faced many challenges. Before he was 18 years old, his mother died, and years later, his father abandoned him and his siblings. Without the nurturing care of his mother and masculine guidance from his father, Phillip had to find his own way.

In the mid 1930's, dust storms were a severe problem that affected the agricultural industry in the United States. Dust storms eroded the soil which impaired farmers ability to grow crops and depleted soil-rich natural resources that affected the nation's environmental health. To combat the problem, on April 27, 1935, President Franklin D. Roosevelt signed the Soil Conservation Act to combat soil erosion and preserve natural resources. The act also established the Soil Conservation Service to engage in research, preventive-based activities involving soil erosion and natural resources preservation. A year later, on February 29, 1936, the Soil Conservation and Allotment Act, paid farmers to plant native plants, grasses, legumes to support the soil, rather than commercial crops which exhausted the soil nutrients. Seizing the opportunity, Phillip concentrated his efforts towards soil conservation resulting in many accomplishments. Interesting enough, he did not have a college degree nor completed high school. He possessed the intelligence to learn the craft of soil conservation and applied the knowledge.

When African American history is celebrated, little is paid attention to successful African American farmers especially those who participated in soil conservation. Phillip story, including other stories of African Americans, should be recognized to shed light on the historic contributions of African Americans soil conservationists.

VII. From "Isaac and Charlotte Quattlebaum: Former Slaves Who Lived Victoriously"

Seeing his mother sold before his eyes was a traumatizing event for Isaac. Without the nurturing care of his mother; as a child, he had to embody resiliency. His resilience throughout his enslavement served as a foundation for his spiritual growth and adulthood. Resiliently, Isaac lived his life by embodying purposeful living. Refusing to accept his wife Charlotte inability to cook, he taught her. During the infancy of Smyrna Baptist Church, he accepted the call of deaconship. Refusing to accept a lot of sharecropping, he became a landowner. Recognizing the utility of nature, he owned and operated a syrup mill.

As a syrup mill owner, Isaac religiously practiced bartering by accepting syrup jugs from his customers instead of money; in return, he gave them syrup. Bartering is a system of exchange between parties using good and services instead of currency. During slavery, slaves frequently bartered with each other. Many slaves created bartering entrepreneurial enterprises such as selling agricultural and domestic products such as fruits, vegetables, livestock, clothes. As a former slave, Isaac was exposed to bartering and incorporated in his business.

Although slave communities did not have a system of currency exchange for sustainability, bartering was a venerable system for them. While historically and contemporary capitalism has produced widespread economic depravity among African Americans ascribed by racism, poverty, and limited channels of wealth accessibility, but in some enslave communities, bartering circumvented economic depravity. The continuous conversation about economic depravity among African Americans must be broadened beyond racial capitalism and more focused on economic security strategies such as bartering. Since economic security is primarily focused on materialistic acquisition and possessiveness, a bartering system such as bartering food, clothes, transportation, real estate, or even currency can potentially decrease economic depravity among African Americans as well as other communities.

Charlotte, who mother was sold; as a child, too had to embody resiliency. Without the nurturing care and guidance of her mother, womanhood certainly was a challenge. Although her emotive personality was fiery, it was Charlotte who became a "mother figure" to her siblings and relatives alike. She not only raised her children, but also her young siblings, who were around the same ages of her children. In addition, Charlotte was the firstborn "Thompson," older than all her siblings and first cousins, according to genealogical record.

The descendants of Isaac and Charlotte were civically active in the early days of Smyrna Missionary Baptist Church serving as deacons, trustees, and other roles. Isaac himself was a deacon and the tradition of the Quattlebaum family serving in the church is legendary. Even today, the Quattlebaum family is still actively involved in Smyrna and in other local and non-local churches.

According to Molefi Asante (1988), "There are two aspects of consciousness (1) toward oppression and (2) toward victory" (50). Despite being former slaves who lived in the Jim Crow era of pervasive and severe racial discrimination, they chose to inculcate a victorious consciousness. Their lives should serve as a reminder that nothing is impossible; but inculcating victorious consciousness open vantages toward purposeful living.

According to Molefi Asante (1988), "There are two aspects of consciousness (1) toward oppression and (2) toward victory" (50).[104] Despite being former slaves who lived in the Jim Crow era of pervasive and severe racial discrimination, they chose to inculcate a victorious consciousness. Their lives should serve as a reminder that nothing is impossible; but inculcating victorious consciousness open vantages toward purposeful living.

VIII. From "Lavinia Corley Thompson: South Carolina African American Female Confederate Veteran"

On the fall of 1861, the great abolitionist Frederick Douglass wrote, "It is now pretty well established, that there are at the present moment many colored men in the Confederate army doing duty not only as cooks, servants and laborers, but as real soldiers, having muskets on their shoulders, and bullets in their pockets, ready to shoot down loyal troops, and do all that soldiers may to destroy the Federal Government and build up that of the traitors and rebels. There were such soldiers at Manassas, and they are there still."[105] Douglass, along with many others, verified the existence of African Americans who served in the Confederate army. Both enslaved and freemen served dutifully in various capacities in the Confederate army throughout the war.

---

[104] Asante, Molefi. *Afrocentricity: The Theory of Social Change*. African American Images/Africa World Press, 1988, p.50.

[105] Dudley Taylor Cornish. *The Sable Arm: Negro Troops in the Union Army, 1861-1865* (1956).

Lavinia role as cook in her Confederate regiment should not be ignored. Regimental cooks an integral role in their unit military operations. Cooks had to display ingenuity in preparing food for soldiers in both pleasant and unpleasant circumstances. Some soldiers conversate with cooks about their personal lives and interests.

As of date, Lavinia is the only African American Female Confederate Pensioner recognized in the state of South Carolina. She, as well as ten African-American men from Aiken County, are in an elite club of over 100 African-Americans who are Confederate Pensioners.[106] [107] In addition, her story is sublime like other African-Americans Confederate veterans like Charles Hayes and Samuel Lee, two of the three founders of Aiken County.[108] She may not have taken up arms, but her life was placed in just as much jeopardy and she suffered from the same hardships as the regular soldiers.

IX. From "Oscar J. Thompson, Sr.: From Sharecropper to Entrepreneur"

Booker T. Washington (1909) quoted, "Freedom, in the larger and higher sense, every man must gain for himself" (222). Extricating himself from the uncertainties of sharecropping life, Oscar gained his freedom by becoming an entrepreneur. First, he acquired land. Then, he leveraged the land for economic opportunities.

Oscar's agricultural pursuits are noteworthy. His employment of the three-year crop rotation demonstrated his inventiveness. As a member of the delegation of African American farmers visiting Coker Pedigreed Farm, demonstrated Oscar's zealously to stay abreast educationally in the field of agriculture. He understood the importance

---

[106] Helsley, Jones Alexia, *South Carolina's African American Confederate Pensioners 1923-1925.*

[107] Other African American Confederate pensioners from Aiken County were Emmet Barret, Elliot Gass, Will Gantt, Alex Harrison, Ansell Kelly, Charlie Neal, Frank Prophet, Hort Quarles, Sank Wigfall, and Alex Williams.

[108] Vandervelde, Isabel (1999). *Aiken County: The Only South Carolina founded during Reconstruction.* Spartanburg: Reprint Co.

of leveraging opportunities in agricultural by taking risks, being inventive, and acquiring necessary knowledge. Oscar's real estate ventures demonstrated his zeal to see some of his relatives to become landowners. I suspected that he wanted them to enjoy the pleasures of landownership. Furthermore, he profited!

Without a college degree, Oscar demonstrated that having the "will" to become successful is imperative. He was not satisfied just being a sharecropper, he destined for something greater, something better. Despite living in the Jim Crow era, he became a successful entrepreneur overcoming whatever odds he faced. I suspected that Oscar knew the criticality of economic opportunities, especially in an era where economic opportunities for rural southern African Americans were limited.

Even in contemporary times, economic opportunities among African Americans are limited, but can be exponential if entrepreneurship is fully embraced. Although racism will continue to adversely impact economic opportunities, entrepreneurship is the only factor that African Americans can employ to survive economically. Oscar knew that landownership, agriculture, and real estate were his entrepreneurial keys that unlocked the door to extrapolate wealth.

X. From "Joshua and Queen Thompson-Corley: Symbolic Figures of Grittiness"

Like many formerly enslaved people who included Joshua and Queen parents, they had to contemplate ways to survive in a racial polarized, capitalistic society. Lacking proper education and guidance, some formerly enslaved people had no choice except oblige into a servitude life. The economic elites, which included former slave masters, knew that many formerly enslaved people could not secure economic freedom or living for themselves. As a result, the economic elites formulated the sharecropping system, that afforded formerly enslaved people including poor Whites the opportunity to earn money. Sharecropping required persons (sharecroppers) to live on the landowner property; in return, sharecroppers must farm the land and

44

produce enough "crop" satisfactory to the landowner or face punitive consequences such as lifetime debt or eviction from the landowners' property.

As sharecroppers, Joshua and Queen had to deal with the circumstances of the times. The long toil of sharecropping, the demanding requirements of the landowners, and raising their children in Jim Crow South was arduous indeed. Faced with daunting circumstances, they exhibited a victorious consciousness throughout their lives. Their impeccable moral and spiritual virtues, sense of humor, and their devotion to the Christian faith, were imperative throughout their lives. Furthermore, they sacrificed for the well-being of their children.

What is noteworthy is Queen's chastising the wealthy landowner who, because of the thinness of the crop, wanted more of his fair share. There are countless stories of sharecroppers and their families who were forced to work more than required, regardless of their health conditions. Most sharecroppers were denied legal protections and there were no unions to advocate for decent wages. Nevertheless, Queen demonstrated courage by evocating a moral position believing that her children's welfare was far important than obliging the wealthy landowner. Mistreatment of sharecroppers was one of several precursor events that defined the American Labor movement. The movement grew up out of the need to protect the common interests of labor that included better wages, safer working conditions, and reasonable hours. Although most historical accounts of the American Labor movement focused on urban areas, there is paucity of historical accounts focused on the nefarious and immoral exploitation of sharecroppers. Queen's evocation is a prime example.

With little material wealth, Joshua and Queen's legacy lives among their descendants. Their sacrifice allowed many of their descendants to pursue professional and notable blue-collar occupations too numerous to identify. The adage holds true, "It's not where you start, but where you finished." Joshua and Queen started out as sharecroppers; but finished their lives as venerable progenitors.

BILIOGRAPHY

"1930; Census Place: Washington, District of Columbia; Page: 13B; Enumeration District: 0256; Digital Image." Digital image. Ancestry.com. Accessed June 10, 2018. www.ancestry.com.

"Activities Among Colored Aikenites and Vicinity." The Journal and Review (Aiken, South Carolina), May 15, 1935. www.newspapers.com.

"Aiken County News Notes." The Journal and Review (Aiken, South Carolina). www.newspapers.com.

"Aiken Farmers Receive Awards of Merit for '42." Aiken Standard and Review (Aiken, South Carolina), February 10, 1943. www.newspapers.com.

"Attempted Murder at Kitchings Mill." The Journal and Review (Aiken, South Carolina). www.newspapers.com.

Birth Certificate for John W. Quattlebaum, 12 October 1942, South Carolina Delayed Birth Records (1766-1900) and City of Charleston, South Carolina Birth Records (1877-1901), Www.ancestry.com.

"Boys Dies 0f Wounds." The Journal and Review (Aiken, South Carolina). www.newspapers.com.

"Civil War Service Records, Confederate Records," Digital Images, Fold3, Fifteenth (Lucas') Battalion Pg. 1-4, Entry for S.G.B Webb, Www.Fold3.com." Digital image.

"Civil War Service Records, Confederate Records," Digital Images, Fold3, 1st Local Troops Infantry, Pg. 1-5, Entry for Samuel G. Webb, Www.Fold3.com." Digital image.

"The Colony." Aiken Standard (Aiken, South Carolina), January 10, 1945. www.newspapers.com.

"Colored News By Home and Farm Agents." Aiken Standard (Aiken, South Carolina), June 30, 1943. www.newspapers.com.

"County and Home Agents Discuss Advantages of Victory Gardens." Aiken Standard and Review (Aiken, South Carolina). www.newspapers.com.

"County News." Aiken Standard and Review (Aiken, South Carolina), March 31, 1943. www.newspapers.com.

Death Certificate for Charlotte Quattlebaum, 19 January 1940, File No. 1810, State of South Carolina, Bureau of Vital Statistics, State Board of Heath, Www.ancestry.com.

Death Certificate for George Piper, 13 March 1921, File No. 18351, State of South Carolina, Bureau of Vital Statistics, State Board of Heath, Www.ancestry.com.

Death Certificate for Governor Logan Thompson, Jr., 28 June 1921, File No. 18352, State of South Carolina, Bureau of Vital Statistics, State Board of Heath, Www.ancestry.com.

Death Certificate for Isaac Quattlebaum, March 1922, File No. 4725, State of South Carolina, Bureau of Vital Statistics, State Board of Heath, Www.ancestry.com.

Death Certificate for Joseph Thompson, 20 February 1949, File No. C1114, State of South Carolina, Bureau of Vital Statistics, State Board of Heath, Www.ancestry.com.

Death Certificate for Lessie Thompson, 21 September 1949, File No. 013591, State of South Carolina, Bureau of Vital Statistics, State Board of Heath, Www.ancestry.com.

Death Certificate for Levinie Thompson, 8 June 1928, File No. 9632, State of South Carolina, Bureau of Vital Statistics, State Board of Heath, Www.ancestry.com.

Death Certificate for Oscar J. Thompson, 11 August 1945, File No. 08484, State of South Carolina, Bureau of Vital Statistics, State Board of Heath, Www.ancestry.com.

Death Certificate for Phillip Thompson, 17 August 1956, File No. 009771, State of South Carolina, Bureau of Vital Statistics, State Board of Heath, Www.ancestry.com.

Death Certificate for Queen Corley, 17 January 1952, File No. 000012, State of South Carolina, Bureau of Vital Statistics, State Board of Heath, Www.ancestry.com.

Death Certificate for Sustanchia Thompson, 19 September 1957, File No. 12947, State of South Carolina, Bureau of Vital Statistics, State Board of Heath, Www.ancestry.com.

Deed of Sale from Bertie Rice to Oscar Thompson, 4 October 1916 (recorded 29 November 1916) Deed Book 26, Page 307, Aiken County Grantee Index Conveyance Book, O-Z, South Carolina Department of Archives and History.

Deed of Sale from Claudia Brodie Et.al to Isaac Quattlebaum and Harvey Quattlebaum, 23 February 1901 (recorded 17 June 1901),

Deed Book 11-1, Page 215, Aiken County Grantee Index Conveyance Book, O-Z, South Carolina Department of Archives and History.

Deed of Sale from David Link to Oscar Thompson, 9 December 1915 (recorded 18 January 1916), Deed Book 25, Page 172, Aiken County Grantee Index Conveyance Book, O-Z, South Carolina Department of Archives and History.

Deed of Sale from Oscar Thompson to Keller Thompson, 12 August 1918 (recorded 15 August 1918) Deed Book 29, Page 334, Aiken County Grantee Index Conveyance Book, O-Z, South Carolina Department of Archives and History.

Deed of Sale from Vianna Corbett Et.al to Oscar Thompson, 23 December 1919 (recorded 24 December 1919) Deed Book 34, Page 119, Aiken County Grantee Index Conveyance Book, O-Z, South Carolina Department of Archives and History.

Dubois, W.E.B. The Souls of Black Folk. New York: Barnes & Noble Classic, 1903.

"Farming Practices Paying Off." The Journal and Review (Aiken, South Carolina), April 28, 1952. www.newspapers.com.

Gantt, Samuel, and Jacqueline Carter. "Oral Interview." Interview by author. November 12, 2017.

"General Sessions Court Convened." Aiken Standard, September 28, 1921. www.newspapers.com.

"Governor Thompson Shoots George Piper to Death Near Kitchings Mill," The Journal and Review (Aiken, South Carolina), March 16, 1921. www.newspapers.com.

Helsley, Alexia Jones. South Carolina's African-American Confederate Pensioners 1923-1925. South Carolina Department of Archives and History, 1998.

In-person Conversation with Artee Quattlebaum Brown. June 15, 2008. Artee Residence, Salley, South Carolina.

In-person Conversation with Catherine Seawright McCollough. 1996. Catherine Residence, Salley, South Carolina.

In-person Conversation with Floster T. Ellison, Jr. January 15, 2004. Floster Residence, Colmubia, South Carolina.

In-person Conversation with Otis Corbitt. January 15, 2004. Otis Residence, Columbia, South Carolina.

Jackson, Annie Laurel Quattlebaum. "Oral Interview." Interview by author. July 1, 2016.

"Local Brevites." Aiken Standard (Aiken, South Carolina), November 29, 1922. www.newspapers.com.

"Luke Rodgers Recovering." Aiken Standard (Aiken, South Carolina), November 15, 1922. www.newspapers.com.

Molefi, Asante. Afrocentricity: The Theory of Social Change. African American Images/Africa World Press, 1988.

"Negro Farmers Visit Coker Seed Plant." Aiken Standard and Review (Aiken, South Carolina), August 9, 1944. www.newspapers.com.

"Negro Wounds Wagener Police." Aiken Standard, October 25, 1922. www.newspapers.com.

Pension application for Lavina Thompson, Records of the Comptroller General, Pension Applications, 1919-1926, #496. South Carolina Department of Archives and History.

The Quattlebaum Family Reunion Booklet. July 1985.

"Rack" Odom Gets Life Sentence for Killing Colored Boy-Fallaw Must Open Road." The Journal and Review (Aiken, South Carolina), October 12, 1921. www.newspapers.com.

"Real Estate Transfers." The Journal and Review (Aiken, South Carolina), October 17, 1943. www.newspapers.com.

Seigler, Robert S. South Carolina's Military Organizations during the War between the States. Charleston: History Press, 2008.

"Soil Conservation." The Journal and Review (Aiken, South Carolina), February 17, 1943. www.newspapers.com.

Thompson, Bernard. "Oral Interview." Telephone interview by author. November 11, 2016.

The Thompson Family Reunion Book. July 1987.

"Three Convicts Escape." The Journal and Review (Aiken, South Carolina), May 9, 1923. www.newspapers.com.

Timber Title from John Friday and Otis Thompson to Aiken Lumber Company, Title Book No.75, P.243, September 10, 1940. Clerk of Court for Aiken County, Aiken County, South Carolina.

APPENDIX A-PICTURES

Milledge Thompson Family Home

From the far left on the porch: Charlotte T. Quattlebaum, Nathan Thompson, Sr., Louise T. Kitchings, Bannon Thompson, Acklin T. Hunt, Nancy T. Johnson, Gussie T. Staley, and Lena T. Frazier. **From the far left on the ground:** Bessie T. Stroman, Purvis Thompson, Sr., Otis Thompson, Sr., **Milledge Thompson, Amanda F. Thompson (Milledge's wife)**, Polly T.S. Miles, and Sumpter Thompson.

Otis Thompson, Sr. and his daughter Blanche Thompson-Gantt

Mary Ellen McKie-Thompson, wife of Otis Thompson

Murry Quattlebaum

Governor H. Thompson, Sr.

Joseph Pitts Thompson

Oscar J. Thompson, Sr.

Joshua and Queen T. Corley

APPENDIX B-GRAVE MARKERS

Milledge Thompson grave marker located at Smyrna Baptist
Missionary Church, Springfield, SC.

Otis and Mary Ellen Thompson grave marker located at
Smyrna Missionary Baptist Church, Springfield, SC.

Murry Quattlebaum grave marker located at Smyrna Missionary
Baptist Church, Springfield, SC.

Issac and Charlotte T. Quattlebaum grave marker located at
Smyrna Missionary Baptist Church, Springfield, SC,

Governor Hayes Thompson grave marker located at Smyrna Missionary Baptist Church, Springfield, SC.

Governor "Mint" Thompson, Jr. grave marker at Smyrna
Missionary Baptist Church, Springfield, SC.

Oscar J. and Lessie F. Thompson grave marker located at
Smyrna Missionary Baptist Church, Springfield, SC.

Rev. Logan Thompson, wife of Lavinia C. Thompson, grave marker located at Smyrna Missionary Baptist Church, Springfield, SC.

Lavinia Corley Thompson grave marker located at Smyrna
Baptist Missionary Church, Springfield, SC.

Samuel G. Webb grave marker located at Old White Pond Baptist Church, White Pond, SC.

APPENDIX C-NEWSPAPER ARTICLES

ACTIVITIES AMONG COLORED AIKENITES AND VICINITY

A very large audience witnessed the termination of the Educational Rally at Smyrna Baptist Church on Sunday afternoon, May 12th, for benefit of the schoolhouse at Piney Grove school. The program was given as follows: Spiritual, led by Mr. Otis Thompson, Scripture reading, Rev. Bishop, acting pastor, prayer, Dea. Hilton Johnson, Music, Little Sunshine Band, Remarks and introduction of speaker, Mrs. Evetta Jones. Address, Mr. Mayor Holmes, subject, "Unity" which was very valuable, very instructive and interesting. A public collection of $2.00 was taken at this time followed by reports from, first, the patrons amounting to $30.10, reports from children amounted to $33.07. A check was turned in by Mr. Kennedy amounting to $17.50, amount turned in from present treasurer $3.76. Total amount reported $86.43. The following persons reported the highest amounts in the contests and received prizes: Lillie B. Wooden, crowned as Queen and received first prize for girls, Henry Thompson, crowned as King, and received first prize for boys, Howard Carswell, 2nd prize for boys; Eva M. Williams 2nd prize for girls. First prize for men, Mr. Hamp Sarswell, first prize for ladies, Mrs. Fannie Stroman; 2nd prize Mrs. Mable Woodward. These people are striving to help the county officials build a school house for their children. 118. Their building was burned the past term. We are planning a second rally in the early fall.

Otis Thompson: An individual who had many vocations — Activities Among Colored Aikenites and Vicinity, Aiken, South Carolina, The Journal and Review, 15 May 1935, p.2, www.newspapers.com.

THREE CONVICTS ESCAPE

Three convicts escaped from the Aiken County Chaingang at Whitlaw's Crossing late Sunday night. this camp is located about five miles from Augusta. Rewards have been offered for each one of these men and county officers are optomistic about recapturing them.

One of the convicts, Murray Quattlebaum, as our readers will remember, was the man who shot Officer Luke Rogers at Wagener some time ago. The other who escaped are Press Pinckney and Herbert Lindsey.

Later—Mr. W. B. Brodie, Foreman of the Grand Jury informed us that Murray Quattlebaum turned himself in at Bell's Camp at 3 o'clock Tuesday morning. Quattlebaum said that the other two convicts induced him to escape and after it was over he decided that the best thing for him to do was to go back. He stated that Press Pinckney had been to his aunt at Kitchings Mill to obtain food and that he was going from there to see his mother, who lives on Mr. Brodie's place.

The Vigilante Exploits of Murry Quattlebaum — Three Convicts Escape, Aiken, South Carolina, The Journal and Review, 9 May 1923, p.1, www.newspapers.com.

Local Brevities

Joseph Blackwell has been appointed as policeman in place of Officer Scherer who resigned some time ago.

Murray Quattlebaum, who shot badly and wounded Luke Rodgers Wagener Chief of police, was admitted to bail in the sum of $1,200 last Wednesday before Magistrate Garvin in the Aiken Court house, Mr. Hampton Brodie going on his bond.

The Vigilante Exploits of Murry Quattlebaum — Local Brevites, Aiken, South Carolina, Aiken Standard, 29 November 1922, p.3, www.newspapers.com.

of
Ru-
l Dr.
rook
of
ffair,
clud-
of
are
ndid
and
Civic
af-
ning
elen
onea

———J&R———

LUKE RODGERS RECOVERING

Luke (Doc) Rodgers, the chief of Police of Wagener, who was so seriously wounded by the negro, Murray Quattlebaum, whom he was attempting to arrest, was permitted to leave the Baptist Hospital Saturday and return to his home. Officer Rodgers is still in a very weakened condition from the effects of his wound in the stomach and will be unable to perform his duties as guardian of the peace for some time to come.

The Vigilante Exploits of Murry Quattlebaum — Luke Rodgers Recovering, Aiken, South Carolina, Aiken Standard, 15 November 1922, p.1, www.newspapers.com.

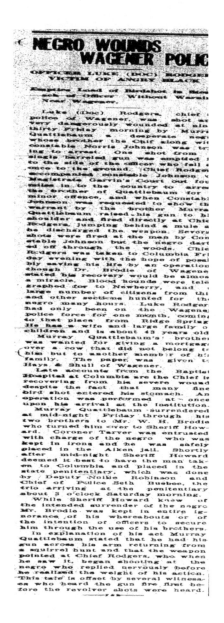

NEGRO WOUNDS WAGENER POLICE

OFFICER LUKE (DOC) RODGERS VICTIM OF ANGRY BLACK

Empties Load of Birdshot in ... ach of Officer Without Warni... Near Wagener.

Luke (Doc) Rodgers, chief ... police of Wagener, was shot a... very dangerously wounded at aln... thirty Friday morning by Murr... Quattlebaum a desperate neg... whose brother the Chie... along wit... Constable Norris Johnson was tr... ing to arrest. One shot from ... single barreled gun was emptied ... to the side of the officer who fell ... once to the ground. Chief Rodge... accompanied constable Johnson ... Magistrate Garvin's Court out fou... miles in to the country to arre... the brother of Quattlebaum for ... minor offence, and when Constabl... Johnson was requested to show th... warrant by the brother Murra... Quattlebaum raised his gun to hi... shoulder and fired directly at Chie... Rodgers, jumping behind a mule a... he discharged the weapon. Severa... shots were fired at the man by Con... stable Johnson but the negro dart... ed off through the woods. Chie... Rodgers was taken to Columbia Fri... day evening with the hope of possi... bly saving his life by an operation ... though Dr. Brodie of Wagene... stated his recovery would be almos... a miracle. Blood hounds were tele... graphed for to Newberry, and ... large number of citizens from thi... and other sections hunted for th... negro many hours. Luke Rodger... had only been on the Wagene... police force for one month, comin... to that place from Ridge Spring... He has a wife and large family o... children and is about 43 years old ... Murray Quattlebaum's brothe... was wanted for giving a mortgag... over a cow that did not belong t... him but to another member of hi... family. The paper was given t... Hays & Shull of Wagener. ... Late accounts from the Baptis... Hospital at Columbia are the Chief i... recovering from his severe woun... despite the fact that many fine ... bird shot entered his stomach. An ... operation was performed at once ... upon his arrival at the institution. ... Murray Quattlebaum surrendered ... at mid-night Friday through his ... two brothers to Mr. W. H. Brodie ... who turned him over to Sheriff How... ard. Coroner Tarver was entrusted ... with charge of the negro who was ... kept in irons and he was safely ... placed in the Aiken jail. Shortly ... after mid-night Sheriff Howard ... deemed it best to have the man tak... en to Columbia and placed in the ... state penitentiary, which was done ... by Deputy Nolke Robinson and ... Chief of Police Seth Busbee, the ... trio arriving at the penitentiary ... about 3 o'clock Saturday morning. ... While Sheriff Howard knew of ... the intended surrender of the negro ... Mr. Brodie was kept in entire ig... norance of his whereabouts or of ... the intention of officers to secure ... him through the use of his brothers. ... In explanation of his act Murray ... Quattlebaum stated that he had his ... gun across his arm returning from ... a squirrel hunt and that the weapon ... pointed at Chief Rodgers, who when ... he saw it, began shooting at the ... negro who replied nervously before ... he realized the weight of his action. ... This tale is offset by several witness... es who heard the gun fire first be... fore the revolver shots were heard.

The Vigilante Exploits of Murry Quattlebaum — Negro Wounds Wagener Police, Aiken, South Carolina, Aiken Standard, 25 October 1922, p.3, www.newspapers.com.

...... a jail term.

The case of Governor Thompson, who is charged with murder, the shooting to death of George Piper in the Kitchings Mill section on the night of March 17th last, was called about noon yesterday. Solicitor Gunter is being aided in the prosecution of the case by William M. Smoak, Esq., and Messrs. Salley and Gyles are attorneys for the defence. Quite an array of witnesses gave testimony yesterday afternoon and it is believed the case will go over into Wednesday.

Tragedy in the Skillet: The murder of Governor "Mint" Thompson, Jr. — General Sessions Court Convened, Aiken, South Carolina, The Journal and Review, Wednesday, September 28, 1921, www.newspapers.com.

BOY DIES OF WOUNDS.

"Governor" Thompson, the 11
ear old negro boy who was recently
hot by a Sniper while sitting at his
ather's table in the Kitchings Mill
ection, died from his wounds Tues-
lay night of last week. From the
irst physicians held out no hope for
iis recovery as the load of shot tore
ι large hole in the child's side.

Tragedy in the Skillet: The murder of young Governor "Mint"
Thompson, Jr. — Boys Dies of Wounds, Aiken, South Carolina,
The Journal and Review, 6 July 1921, p.8,
www.newspapers.com.

ATTEMPTED MURDER AT KITCHINGS MILL

NEGRO BOY GETS SHOT INTENDED FOR FATHER.

"Governor" Thompson's Son Probably Fatally Wounded by Sneaking Sniper While Eating Supper.

The twelve year old son of Governor Thompson, a negro farmer on the place of Mr. John Brodie in the Kitchings Mill section, was probably mortally shot in the back last Saturday night by an unknown party who, it is believed, desired to wreck vengence on the lad's father. It will be recalled that Governor Thompson some time back shot and killed a negro named Piper and is now out on bond to appear for trial in the case. The friends of Piper have been piqued because of Thompson's freedom and it is believed that one of them attempted to shoot him to death in his home last Saturday night. Thompson, who is in the good graces of the white residents of his community, was picked up along the road Saturday night and given a ride to his home. He had scarcely seated himself with his family at the table when the shot from a gun rang out and the younger Thompson fell to the floor with a gaping wound in his back. The gun load passing under the arm of the father to reach the boy. The unknown party had placed the weapon through a crack in the side of the building before he pulled the trigger.

Sheriff Howard and several others answered the call Saturday night and discovered the foot prints of a woman's number 7 shoe. No arrests were made and no further clew could be gained. The authorities and the residents of the Kitchings Mill section were wrought up over the attempted assassination in fear that the parties guilty would not hesitate to strike down others whom they have a grievance against.

Later Sheriff Howard yesterday arrested Buck, alias John Odom, a negro, residing about six miles away from where the shooting occurred on Mr. Cynn Cook's place near Salley. A search revealed a pair of woman's shoes that had been recently tramped through the mud, which were hidden underneath his house. The prisoner tried to prove an alibi as to his whereabouts at the time of the shooting but failed utterly in the attempt. It is now in the opinion of the authorities that Odom who bore a bad feeling against Thompson is the party who did the shooting. The woman's shoes and other developments ...

The Fall Term of the Criminal Court adjourned sine die last Friday afternoon at four o'clock, the last case tried being that of "Rack" Odum, who was charged with the killing of Governor Thompson, Jr., on the 28th of last June. The prisoner was found guilty and recommendation to mercy and give a life sentence.

The shooting of the colored lad was done in a stealthy and most cowardly manner. Odum, who wore a pair of woman's shoes, sneaked up to the little cabin of Thompson in Wagener section while the family were at supper, and thrusting his gun through a crack by the window, shot supposedly at the elder Governor Thompson, the load, however mortally wounding his son who sat with him at the table. At first no hint of the murderer was given, but the woman's shoe track led in a circuitous route for some distance to a road where it ended by the murderer entering a waiting buggy. The track of the mule hitched to the vehicle was then taken up; the shoes found in a negro cabin, and gradually the chain of circumstancial evidence wound firm around "Rack Odum." The trial began Wednesday and lasted until Friday afternoon, twenty-nine witnesses for the State and 14 for the defence being sworn. Hon. John F. Williams assisted the Solicitor and W. M. Smoak, Esq., acted for the defence. Following was the jury: H. C. Weeks, foreman; Claude Cumbee, J. O. Lybrand, G. W. Plunkett, B. K. Boylston, B. G. Hall, T. W. Cummings, R. L. Holsonbake, Lewis Adams, J. E. Bryan, George Solomon, T. T. Derrick.

Tragedy in the Skillet: The murder of young Governor "Mint" Thompson, Jr. — "Rack" Odom Gets Life Sentence for Killing Colored Boy-Fallaw Must Open Road, Aiken, South Carolina, The Journal and Review, 12 October 1921, p.1, www.newspapers.com.

Aiken County News Notes

WAGENER.

Cor. Journal and Review:

A glaring case of cold-blooded, premeditated murder was enacted in the Kitchings Mill section of the county a few nights ago. The intended victim was evidently Governor Thompson, Sr., a prosperous colored man who lives with Mr. J. W. Brodie but the real victim was the eleven year old son of Governor Thompson Thompson had just come home from Mr. Brodie's store, and seated himself at the dining able with his family, who were eating supper, the little boy sitting with his back to the one window in the dining room, and Thompson facing the window across the table from the boy. About the time Thompson took his seat a load of number four bird shot was fired through a small crack in the window, the entire load taking effect in the back of the boy. The boy was mortally wounded and died the next afternoon. Tracks leading from the dining room window, which were followed by the Sheriff and several of the neighbors, next morning together with other circumstantial evidence indicated strongly that the deed was committed by John Henry Odom, otherwise known as "Rack" Odom, colored. The evidence also showed that the murderer was trying to kill Governor Thompson and not his boy.

Warrenville.

Mr. Frampton Willi
Tracy McCarty spent
with Mr. Frank Garla
Mr. and Mrs. Wayk
Warrenville, visited w
Mrs. M. B. Attaway h
Mr. and Mrs. Jim I
stead, Fla. accompa
Redd's mother of K(
were her for a few d:
way to the mountains.
Mr. and Mrs. Cornw
several young people
on last Saturday night
Mr. and Mrs. Otis
tained with a family.
their home on Monday
present were: Mr. and
Mills, and Mrs. Hatt!
and two children of
Mr. and Mrs. Olive G
Mrs. R. J. Wade, Mr. F
Mrs J.m Woodward :
Scott.

NORTH AUG

Mrs. James A. Whit.
Lizzie Rambo honored
Mr. Ben L. Rambo, wi
spend-the-day party at
last Wednesday. celebr
birthday. there being s!
party. Mrs. T. J. Bri:
also Mrs. J. C. Talber

Tragedy in the Skillet: The murder of young Governor "Mint" Thompson, Jr. — Aiken County News Notes, Aiken, South Carolina, The Journal and Review, 6 July 1921, p.8, www.newspapers.com.

Governor Thompson Shoots George Piper to Death Near Kitchings Mill.

Another killing was done last Sunday at midnight as the result of illicit liquor drinking. George Piper, member of an industrious and well-to-do negro family, was shot twice and instantly killed by Governor Thompson, who had but recently attended church services with Piper. From the Sheriff it was learned that Piper became wildly intoxicated from moonshine last Sunday and began shooting up the neighborhood of the Chapman colored Baptist Church in the Kitchings Mill section. He went so far as to shoot in to his father's house in his drunken frenzy. Thompson, it is said, took Piper to task for his conduct and the man turned on him in an effort to shoot him, but Thompson shot first, the balls hitting Piper in the mouth and breast. Monday Thompson surrendered to the Sheriff at the Court House being taken there by Mr. John D. Brodie.

Tragedy in the Skillet: The murder of young Governor "Mint" Thompson, Jr. — Governor Thompson Shoots George Piper to Death Near Kitchings Mill, Aiken, South Carolina, The Journal and Review, 16 March 1921, p.1, www.newspapers.com.

84

Jackson, Hamp Carswell, Broadus
Holmes & Wife, G. A. Kenner &
Wife, Josiah Whack, Chris
Thompson, Mack Livingston &
Wife, Matthew Davenport &
Wife, Paul Kenner, Phillip
Thompson, Rev. John Garrett &
Wife, Henry E. Craig, Nathan
Salley, Eustis Craig and Wife,
John Morgan, Frank Morgan, An-
derson Carter, E. W. Lawrie, No-
lia Kennedy & Husband, Pickens
Miles, P. H. Isaac, Effie B. John-
son, Australia & Fred Crosland.

Phillip Thompson: From sharecropper to soil conservationist.
— Aiken Farmers Receive Awards of Merit for '42, Aiken, South
Carolina, Aiken Standard and Review, 10 February 1943, p.1 and
p.3, www.newspapers.com.

Kudzu is one of the most valuable and general purpose crops that one may plant on the farm and be used for any of the following purposes: a soil builder, a hay crop, a temporary grazing crop, an erosion controller, or as a money crop. or most of the above reasons the following farmers are planting kudzu this year.

Arthur Bell 4 acres, Arthur Bradley 2 acres, Lewie Bynum 2 acres, Hampton Burd, 2 acres, Hasker Cadle 1 acre, Homer Burris 4 acres, Dugar Chavous 2 acres, G. L. Crawford 2 acres, Eddie Davis 2 acres, Matthew Fells 2 acres, Gracy. B. Gantt 6 acres, Goldman Harvey 2 acres, C. C. Johnson 1 acre, Leon Johnson 3 acres, Salley Kenner 2 acres, Alvin Ligons 2 acres, George Meacham 5 acres, Regina Morgan 2 acres, John E. Raiford 2 acres. Ben Peterson 2 acres Elisha Smith 2 acres, Phillip Thompson 2 acres; Total 54 acres.

Phillip Thompson: From sharecropper to soil conservationist — County News, Aiken, South Carolina, Aiken Standard and Review, 31 March 1943, p.6, www.newspapers.com.

Terrace lines have been run on Phillip Thompson's farm near Salley. He says, "the two horse plow loaned him by the Edisto Soil Conservation District does a good job of constructing T terraces. He is planting Kobe Lespedeza for pasture on three acres of his five acre fenced and planned pasture.

New York Original 'Dixie'

Phillip Thompson: From sharecropper to soil conservationist — County and Home Agents Discuss Advantages of Victory Gardens, Aiken Standard and Review, 12 March 1943, p.2, www.newspapers.com.

SOIL CONSERVATION NEWS

Sericea land preparation has been completed on the farm of Phillip Thompson near Salley, S. C. Mr. Thompson is planning to plant about three acres of sericea this coming spring. This area will be used for permanent hay requirements and will serve as a labor saver to the farmer by not having to plow land for hay when this labor is needed elsewhere on the farm.

Phillip Thompson: From sharecropper to soil conservationist — The Colony, Aiken Standard, 10 January 1945, p.8, www.newspapers.com.

Phillip Thompson of Salley has recently cultivated his spring planted kudzu by plowing out the middles in order to keep down the weeds. He also plowed up his terraces for the summer and is planning to plant peas on them to keep down weeds and to prevent the heavy rains from doing any harm to his farm. Phillip continues to brag about educating his hogs to eat Kobe lespedeza which he planted in a fenced pasture last spring for them. He must have enough kobe to keep the hogs eating instead of rooting.

Phillip Thompson: From sharecropper to soil conservationist — Colored News By Home and Farm Agents, Aiken, South Carolina, Aiken Standard, 30 June 1943, p.8, www.newspapers.com.

Farm Practices Paying Off

As a portion of the Cooperative Agreement between the Aiken Soil Conservation District and the Farmer; Otis McCloud, Phillip Thompson, Donald Quattlebaum and Julia S. Woodward, recently finished constructing the terraces on their farms under the supervision of H. J. Hardy, Soil Conservationist for Aiken County, South Carolina.

These terraces were of the broad base type and will meet P.M.A. specifications of seven square feet of channel carrying capacity of water.

Outlets into the woods, for these terraces, were also constructed and where needed, special waterways were made to carry off the excess water. The waterways and fields borders on these farms were planted to sericea to minimize the degree of erosion.

On the four farms, about eight miles of terraces were constructed to help hold the soil in place and is one of the many conservation practices to be carried out on these farms.

"Terrace maintenance, and practices which should be done at least twice a year," says, J. H. Robinson

Phillip Thompson: From sharecropper to soil conservationist — Farming Practices Paying Off, Aiken, South Carolina, The Journal and Review, 28 April 1952, p.2, www.newspapers.com.

Oscar Thompson to Henry and
Eliza Felder 42 acres in Rocky
Grove Township for $775.

Oscar J. Thompson, Sr.: From sharecropper to entrepreneur. —
Real Estate Transfers, Aiken, South Carolina, The Journal and
Review, 17 October 1943, p.3, www.newspapers.com.

A good idea of a three year strip rotation can be seen on Oscar Thompson's farm near Springfield.

Oscar J. Thompson, Sr.: From sharecropper to entrepreneur — Soil Conservation, Aiken, South Carolina, The Journal and Review, 17 February 1943, p.2, www.newspapers.com.

NEGRO FARMERS VISIT COKER SEED PLANT

T. A. Hammond Aiken County Negro Agricultural Agent carried a large group of farmers to Cokers Pedigreed Farm, Hartsville last Thursday to study and observe seed breeding and other farm practices.

The farmers noted many new farming ideas, that will benefit them. Farmers who had not used the improved cotton seed are planning to use them another year.

Farmers who made the trip were: Henry Craig, Eustis Craig, Lucious Brayboy, Arthur Kenner, Milton Bradley, Clyde Blassingale, Daniel Watson, Lawrence Marshall, John Raiford, Homer Cummings, Homer Cummings Jr., Hasker Cadle, Roddy Burris, Homer Burris, Mack Livingston, Eddie Davis, Johnie William, Sam Gantt, Robert Friday, Bennie Tyler, Oscar Thompson, Tim Tyler, and others whose names were not recorded.

Agent T. A. Hammond has been in the Extension field and in Aiken County since February 1, 1944 and is very pleased with the interest and cooperation of the Aiken County Negro Farmers.

IN MEMORIAM

In Memory of our Son and father.

John Henry James, who departed this life August 4 1941.

Oscar J. Thompson, Sr.: From sharecropper to entrepreneur — Negro Farmers Visit Coker Seed Plant, Aiken, South Carolina, 9 August 1944, p.8, www.newspapers.com.

APPENDIX D-OSCAR J. THOMPSON, SR.
REAL ESTATE DEEDS

(Note: The transcription of the deeds was done by Tonya Browder of the Old Edgefield Genealogical Society)

The State of South Carolina KNOW ALL MEN BY THESE PRESENTS, that I David Link of Deland in the district of Florida in consideration of the sum of one hundred Dollars to me in hand paid at and before the sealing of these Presents by Oscar Thompson of Aiken County in the State of South Carolina the receipt whereof I hereby acknowledge, have granted, bargained, sold and released, and by these Presents DO GRANT, bargain, sell and release unto the said Oscar Thompson

All my interest in my Father's [illegible]

All my interest in certain piece parcel or tract of land situated lying and being in the State of South Carolina County of Aiken containing ninety-two (92) acres more or less Bounded as follows:
North by lands of J. D. Johnson
East by lands of John Corley
South by lands of David Blassengale
West by lands of John Hallman

The Said tract of land being the Same purchased by him of L. R. Hallman
TOGETHER with all and singular the Rights, Members, Hereditaments and Appurtenances to the said Premises belonging, or in anywise incident or appertaining TO HAVE AND TO HOLD, all and singular, the said premises before mentioned unto the said Oscar Thompson Heirs and Assigns forever.

And I do hereby bind myself my Heirs, Executors and Administrators to warrant and forever defend all and singular unto the said Oscar Thompson his Heirs and Assigns, against myself and my Heirs and all Persons whatsoever lawfully claiming or to claim the same or any part thereof.
WITNESS my Hand and Seal, this [blank] day of [blank] in the year of our Lord one thousand nine hundred and fifteen and in the one

hundred and 39th year of the Sovereignty and Independence of the United States of America.

Signed, Sealed and Delivered} David Link
In the Presence of}
Hazel E. Myers
N. Y. Davis
THE STATE OF FLORIDA
County of [blank]

Personally appeared before me Hazel Meyers and made oath that Eda Link wife of the within named David Link sign, seal and as her act and deed, deliver the within written Deed, and that she with N. Y. Davis witnessed the completion thereof.
SWORN to before me, this 9th day of December A. D. 1915

Taurence Thompson
Notary Public
Recorded January 18, 1916

The State of South Carolina, KNOW ALL MEN BY THESE PRESENTS, that I Oscar Thompson in the State aforesaid in consideration of the sum of Two Hundred ($200.00) to me in hand paid at and before the sealing of these Presents by Keller Thompson in the State aforesaid (the receipt whereof is hereby acknowledged), have granted, bargained, sold and released, and by these Presents DO GRANT, sell and release unto the said Keller Thompson, her Heirs and Assigns:

All that tract of land in Aiken County, South Carolina, containing Twenty Two (22) Acres, and being Out of from the Western portion of that tract of land recently purchased by me at Master's Sale in an action entitled Oscar Thompson, Etal, vs. Lonnie Gardone?, Etal Said Parcel of land being Bounded on the North by lands of J. Halman,

Estate, to the East by lands of Oscar Thompson, to the South by lands of Daniel Blasingall and to the West by lands of Mrs. Leila May Brooke. It is expected that the property hereby conveyed is to contain Twenty Two (22) and that within a reasonable time the acres of the said parcel shall be run off by a competent surveyor, a plat made, and that the plat so made by him shall bear the initials of the parties to this deed and shall then constitute a part of this conveyance. The property is conveyed in lieu of any demonstrative case that the grantee herein may have been entitled action and in full of all demands in connection with the property involved in Said on the part of the grantee against one or any other tenant in common.

And I do hereby bind myself, my Heirs, Executors and Administrators to warrant and forever defend all and singular unto the said Keller Thompson her Heirs and Assigns, against me and my Heirs and all others lawfully claiming or to claim the same or any part thereof.

WITNESS my hand and seal this 12th day of April in the year of our Lord one thousand nine hundred and [blank] and in the one hundred and [blank] year of the Sovereignty and Independence of the United States of America.

Signed, Sealed and Delivered } Oscar Thompson
in the Presence of }
Ernest L. Allen
P. F. Henderson
The State of South Carolina }
County of Aiken }

Personally appeared before me Ernest L. Allen and made oath that he saw the within named Oscar Thompson Sign, Seal and as his act and deed, deliver the within written Deed, and that he with P. F. Henderson witnessed the execution thereof.
Sworn to before me, this 12th day of }

August A. D. 1918   }   Ernest L. Allen

(Seal) P. F. Henderson N. P. S. C.

THE STATE OF SOUTH CAROLINA   RENUNCIATION OF DOWER COUNTY OF AIKEN

I, P. F. Henderson, Notary Public, South Carolina, do hereby certify unto all whom it may concern that Mrs. Lessie Thompson the wife of the within named Oscar Thompson did this day appear before me and upon being privately and separately examined by me, did declare that she does freely, voluntarily, and without any compulsion, dread or fear of any person or persons whomsoever, renounce, release and forever relinquish unto the within named Keller Thompson, her heirs and assigns, all her interest and estate, and all her right and claim of Dower, or to all and singular the provisions within mentioned and released.

GIVEN, under my Hand and Seal, this 12th day of August A. D. 1918
P. F. Henderson
Lessie Thompson
N. P. S. C.
Recorded August 15th, 1918

The State of South Carolina, Aiken County, KNOW ALL MEN BY THESE PRESENTS, that We Vianna Corbett, Susie Johnson and Ruannah Martin in consideration of the sum of Thirteen Hundred ($1,300.00) Dollars to us in hand paid at and before the sealing of these Presents by Oscar Thompson in the State aforesaid (the receipt whereof is hereby acknowledged), have granted, bargained, sold and released, and by these Presents DO GRANT, sell and release unto the said Oscar Thompson, his heirs and assigns:

All that certain tract or parcel of land situate in Rocky Grove Township, Aiken County, South Carolina, and bounded:

North by lands of John Corley; East by lands of Lawrence Ware, Peter Stroman, and John Corley; South by lands of George L. Sawyer; West by lands of Oscar Thompson and David Blassengale; said tract of land containing forty-two (42) acres, more or less. TOGETHER with all and singular the Rights, Members, Hereditaments and Appurtenances to the said Premises belonging, or in anywise incident or appertaining TO HAVE AND TO HOLD, all and singular, the said premises before mentioned unto the said Oscar Thompson, his Heirs and Assigns forever. And we do hereby bind ourselves and our Heirs, Executors and Administrators, to warrant and forever defend all and singular the said premises unto the said Oscar Thompson, his Heirs and Assigns, against us and our Heirs, and all other persons whomsoever lawfully claiming or to claim the same or any part thereof.

WITNESS our hands and Seals this 23rd day of December in the year of our Lord one thousand nine hundred and nineteen and in the one hundred and 144th year of the Sovereignty and Independence of the United States of America.

Signed, Sealed and Delivered }   Vianna (her X mark) Corbett
in the Presence of   }   Susie (her X mark) Johnson
E. S. Henderson   Ruannah (her X mark) Martin
P. F. Henderson

The State of South Carolina   }
County of Aiken   }
PERSONALLY APPEARED, before me E. S. Henderson and made oath that he saw the within named Vianna Corbett, Susie Johnson and Ruanah Martin, by mark, Sign, Seal and as their act and deed, deliver the within written deed, and that he with P. F. Henderson witnessed the execution thereof.

Sworn to before me, this 23rd day   }
of December A. D. 1919   }   E. S. Henderson

P. F. Henderson (Seal)
Notary Public
Recorded December 24, 1919

The State of South Carolina, Aiken County, KNOW ALL MEN BY THESE PRESENTS, that I Bertie Rice of Arcadia, Desoto County, State of Florida for and in consideration of the sum of One Hundred Dollars to me in hand paid at and before the sealing of these Presents by Oscar Thompson in the State aforesaid (the receipt whereof is hereby acknowledged), have granted, bargained, sold and released, and by these Presents DO GRANT, sell and release unto the said Oscar Thompson:

All my undivided right, Title, and Interest in and To all that certain piece, parcel or Tract of Land Known as the Jacob Rice Estate Situate, Lying and being in the County of Aiken in the State of South Carolina and containing ninety-six (96) acres, More or Less, and Bounded on the North by Lands of M. Johnson, East by Lands of Nina Martin, South by Lands formerly belonging to Mary Rowe, now held by Danial Blassingale and West by Estate Lands of John Holman. TOGETHER with all and singular the Rights, Members, Hereditaments and Appurtenances to the said Premises belonging, or in anywise incident or appertaining TO HAVE AND TO HOLD, all and singular, the said premises before mentioned unto the said Oscar Thompson, his Heirs and Assigns forever.

And I do hereby bind myself and my Heirs, Executors and Administrators, to warrant and forever defend all and singular the said premises unto the said Oscar Thompson, his Heirs and Assigns, against me and my Heirs, and all others whomsoever lawfully claiming or to claim the same or any part thereof.

WITNESS my Hand and Seal this 4th day of October in the year of our Lord one thousand nine hundred and sixteen and in the one

100

hundred and Forty Second year of the Sovereignty and Independence of the United States of America.

Signed, Sealed and Delivered   }   Bertie Rice (Seal)

in the Presence of   }

R. H. Willsford

R. W. Edwards

The State of South Carolina   }

County of Aiken   }

PERSONALLY APPEARED, before me R. S. Willsford and made oath that he saw the within named Bertie Rice, by mark, Sign, Seal and as her act and deed, deliver the within written deed, and that he with R. W. Edwards witnessed the execution thereof.

Sworn to before me, this 4th day   }

of October A. D. 1916   }   R. H. Willsford

R. O. Turner (Seal)

Notary Public Desoto

State of Florida

Recorded November 29, 1916

APPENDIX E-SAM WEBB
CONFEDERATE SERVICE RECORDS

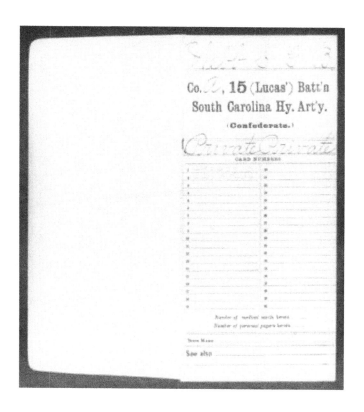

""Civil War Service Records, Confederate Records," Digital Images, Fold3, Fifteenth (Lucas') Battalion Pg. 1-4, Entry for S.G.B Webb, Www.Fold3.com." Digital image.

""Civil War Service Records, Confederate Records," Digital Images, Fold3, Fifteenth (Lucas') Battalion Pg. 1-4, Entry for S.G.B Webb, Www.Fold3.com." Digital image.

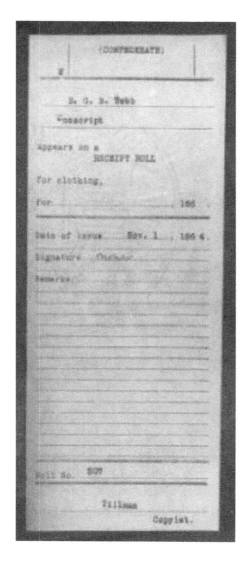

"""Civil War Service Records, Confederate Records," Digital Images, Fold3, Fifteenth (Lucas') Battalion Pg. 1-4, Entry for S.G.B Webb, Www.Fold3.com." Digital image.

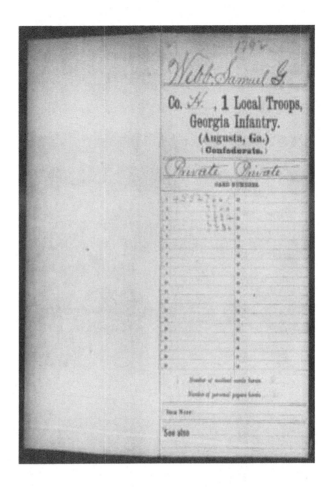

"Civil War Service Records, Confederate Records," digital images, Fold3, 1st Local Troops Infantry, pg. 1-5, entry for Samuel G. Webb, www.Fold3.com.

"Civil War Service Records, Confederate Records," digital images, Fold3, 1st Local Troops Infantry, pg. 1-5, entry for Samuel G. Webb, www.Fold3.com.

"Civil War Service Records, Confederate Records," digital images, Fold3, 1st Local Troops Infantry, pg. 1-5, entry for Samuel G. Webb, www.Fold3.com.

"Civil War Service Records, Confederate Records," digital images, Fold3, 1st Local Troops Infantry, pg. 1-5, entry for Samuel G. Webb, www.Fold3.com.

APPENDIX F-LAVINIA C. THOMPSON SOUTH CAROLINA CONFEDERATE PENSION

State of South Carolina,
County of _Aiken,_

TO THE COUNTY PENSION BOARD:

The undersigned applies for enrollment under the Act of 1923. I served the State of South Carolina in the War between the States, as _Cook_ under _Sam Webb_ who was in Company _A. 1st_ Regiment _of Reserve_ Captain _Hutto_ I went in the service _Sept 1st_ 1863, and served continuously until _End of War_ 1865 remaining faithful to the Confederacy throughout the said war, and my conduct since the war has been such that I am entitled to a pension under the aboveAct. I reside at _In Tabernacle Township_ in _Aiken_ County, S. C.

Sworn to and Subscribed before me this 11th. day

of _May_ 1923

JW Johnson (LS)

Notary Public for South Carolina.

Lavina her X Thompson (age 78y)
Give name in full.
R.F.D #,2, Sally', S.C.

CB B13 Thompson

STATE OF SOUTH CAROLINA,
County of _Barnwell._

Personally appeared before me _Harrison Davis_ and _Jane Anderson,_ and being duly sworn, each of them deposes and says that they know _Lavina Thompson,_ who is an applicant for a pension, and they have read the said application; that they know of their own knowledge that the applicant served the State of South Carolina for more than six (6) months during the War between the States under _Sam Webb,_ and remained faithful to the Confederacy during the said war and that his conduct since then has been such that will entitle him to a pension under the Act of 1923; that the applicant is a resident of the State and resides in _Aiken Co._ County, S. C.

Sworn to before me this 11th. day

of _May,_ 1923

JW Johnson (LS)

Notary Public for South Carolina,

Approved by _JM Cobb_, Chairman Board of Honor, _Aiken County_

County, this 15 day of _May_ 1923

Harrison his X Davis, (age, 75y)
Jane X Anderson (age, 73y)

Pension application for Lavinia Thompson, Records of the Comptroller General, Pension Applications, 1919-1926, #496. South Carolina Department of Archives and History.

ACKNOLWEDGEMENTS

This section of the book acknowledges family members, individuals, and ancillary organizations who contributed to the contents of this book and continuous inspiration for the completion of the book.

Thompson Family Members

Toretha Corley Wright

Clote Gantt-Davis

Annie Laurel Quattlebaum Lloyd Jackson

Christine Quattlebaum Morgan

Robert B. Thompson

Samuel Gantt

Jacqueline Carter

Martha E. Oliver

Individuals

Brenda Baratto, Director, Aiken County Historical Museum

Laura Virgo, Collections Manager, Aiken County Historical Museum

Pete Peters, President of the Aiken-Barnwell Genealogical Society

Tonya Browder, Old Edgefield Genealogical Society

Gloria Wooden-Williams, Retired Educator and member of Smyrna Baptist Church

Organizations

Aiken County Historical Museum

Aiken-Barnwell Genealogical Society

Old Edgefield Genealogical Society

South Carolina Department of Archives and History

ABOUT THE AUTHOR

Walter B. Curry, Jr., Ed.D is a native of Orangeburg, South Carolina. Dr. Curry received a bachelor's degree in political science from South Carolina State University, Orangeburg, SC, in 2003. Dr. Curry earned several graduate degrees in education which includes a doctorate degree in Curriculum and Instruction from Argosy University, Sarasota. He has taught middle school social studies for five years in urban and rural school districts. As a teacher, Dr. Curry served as a Social Studies Department Chair, conducted professional development opportunities for teachers to support school and district-wide initiatives.

Since leaving the classroom, Dr. Curry has matriculated into other ventures. He is an adjunct professor of education at Claflin University teaching undergraduate and graduate courses. In addition, he serves as the administrative coordinator of Project Pipeline Repair, a collaborative initiative with Claflin University, the South Carolina State Commission on Higher Education, and the State Higher Education Executive Officers (SHEEO) to prepare minority high school males to become future educators. Recently, Dr. Curry launched Renaissance Publications, LLC, a self-publishing book company specializing in writing family history through the African American experience.

Dr. Curry is a member of the South Carolina Council for the Social Studies, the South Carolina Association of Teacher Educators, Family Promise of the Midlands, Inc., Richland 2 Black Parents Association, Friends of the Aiken County Historical Museum, The Aiken-Barnwell Genealogical Society, and Lt. General Wade Hampton Camp No.273.

Dr. Curry currently resides in Columbia, South Carolina with his wife Takiyah, and their two sons, Braxton, and Braylon.

Made in the USA
Las Vegas, NV
29 July 2022

52394395R00069